Second Simplicity

Second Simplicity: New Poetry and Prose, 1991–2011

YVES BONNEFOY

SELECTED, TRANSLATED, AND WITH AN INTRODUCTION BY HOYT ROGERS

Yale UNIVERSITY PRESS
NEW HAVEN & LONDON

A MARGELLOS WORLD REPUBLIC OF LETTERS BOOK

The Margellos World Republic of Letters is dedicated to making literary works from around the globe available in English through translation. It brings to the English-speaking world the work of leading poets, novelists, essayists, philosophers, and playwrights from Europe, Latin America, Africa, Asia, and the Middle East to stimulate international discourse and creative exchange.

Yale University Press books may be purchased in quantity for educational, business, or promotional use. For information, please e-mail sales.press@yale.edu (US office) or sales@yaleup.co.uk (UK office).

Set in Electra type by Keystone Typesetting, Inc., Orwigsburg, Pennsylvania.
Printed in the United States of America.

Library of Congress Cataloging-in-Publication Data

Bonnefoy, Yves.
[Poems. English & French. Selections]
Second simplicity : new poetry and prose, 1991–2011 / Yves Bonnefoy ; selected, translated, and with an introduction by Hoyt Rogers.
p. cm. — (The Margellos World Republic of letters)
ISBN 978-0-300-17625-4 (clothbound : alk. paper)
I. Rogers, Hoyt. II. Title.
PQ2603.O533A25 2012
841′.914—dc23 2011038064

A catalogue record for this book is available from the British Library.

This paper meets the requirements of ANSI/NISO Z39.48–1992 (Permanence of Paper).

10 9 8 7 6 5 4 3 2 1

CONTENTS

ACKNOWLEDGMENTS

I would like to thank Jonathan Galassi, Grace Schulman, Richard Howard, Daniel Javitch, Barbara Epler, and Marilyn Hacker for their generous encouragement of this project. Alastair Reid gave me valuable advice on my translations of "America" and "A Childhood Memory of Wordsworth's." Above all, I am grateful to Yves Bonnefoy himself, who sent me most of these pieces over the years even before they were published in France, and who patiently assisted me with points of interpretation, turns of phrase, and clarifications of his sources. Of course, the opinions expressed in the Introduction are entirely my own.

Many of the translations in this volume, as well as portions of the foreword, have already appeared in *Poetry, The Southern Review, AGNI, The Partisan Review, The Yale Review, Nimrod,* the *Spoon River Poetry Review,* the *Cumberland Poetry Review, The Southern Humanities Review, Poetry International, The Kenyon Review,* the *New England Review,* and *Cerise Press.* Like the founders of the Margellos series, the editors of all these reviews deserve our special thanks for supporting literature in translation. "Passerby, these are words . . ." was chosen by Poet Laureate Billy Collins in 2003 for his Random House anthology, *Poetry 180.* The selections from *The Curved Planks* are drawn from the Farrar, Straus, and Giroux edition of 2006, by kind permission. Yves Bonnefoy and I acknowledge the cooperation of Mercure de France and Galilée, which published the French originals printed here; except for a few author's corrections, we have reproduced the punctuation in their editions.

My literary agents, Peter and Amy Bernstein, helped with the final

stage of the proposal. I owe a great debt of thanks to John Donatich of Yale University Press, whose admiration of Bonnefoy has brought this anthology to fruition. Without the thoughtful perseverance of his editorial assistant, Niamh Cunningham, and the astute precision of manuscript editor Laura Jones Dooley, I could never have surmounted the hurdles in my path. Attentive to Bonnefoy's wishes, James Johnson designed the cover, based on an image from the author's illustrated essay *The Hinterland*.

Yves Bonnefoy and I dedicate this book to our revered friend Friedhelm Kemp, in memoriam: "Jener entwerfende Geist, welcher das Irdische meistert, / liebt in dem Schwung der Figur nichts wie den wendenden Punkt."

INTRODUCTION

The Second Simplicity of Yves Bonnefoy

Yves Bonnefoy is often acclaimed as France's greatest living poet. In the course of his long career, he has published six major cycles of verse, several volumes of tales, and a number of collections that fuse various genres. He has steadily produced authoritative essays and full-scale books on literature, aesthetics, and a host of other topics. In recognition of his wide-ranging achievements, he was elected by his peers to succeed Roland Barthes in the Chair of Comparative Poetics at the Collège de France. His work has been translated into scores of languages, and he himself is a celebrated translator of Shakespeare, Yeats, Keats, and Leopardi. In the last decade he has added the European Prize for Poetry of 2006 and the Kafka Prize of 2007 to his extensive list of honors, and he is perennially cited as a leading candidate for the Nobel Prize. Though Yves Bonnefoy will soon attain the age of ninety, his longevity has only heightened his creative powers, as the following sample of his most recent writing attests.

Given the scope of Bonnefoy's output in this current and still evolving phase, a single anthology could never encompass it all; but an attempt in that direction, at least for the poetic oeuvre, has now become imperative. No further compilation has appeared in English since 1995, even though the past two decades have arguably been the most prolific and innovative of his entire lifework. *Second Simplicity* complements the earlier selections edited and translated by Galway Kinnell, Anthony Rudolf, Susanna Lang, Richard Pevear, and John Naughton, among others, and published by Jonathan Cape/

Grossmann, Menard Press, Monument Press, Random House, Ohio University Press, and the University of Chicago Press (for these and subsequent references, see the bibliography below). In passing, I would like to acknowledge the acumen of my predecessors; it has been daunting to follow in their footsteps. In chronological order, the present anthology garners both verse and prose from Bonnefoy's latest period; I have chosen the pieces for their representativeness as well as their diversity. Most of the translations have never appeared in book form until now, and some are printed here for the first time. In addition, the final prose works were only published in France a few months ago; so in that respect, *Second Simplicity* constitutes a joint first edition.

John Naughton and Richard Stamelman have assembled many of Bonnefoy's masterly studies of poetics, Shakespeare, and art history in three substantial volumes of English translations. But Anglo-American readers have remained unfamiliar with his more playful and lyrical experiments in prose: aphorisms, obliquely angled memoirs, prose poems, and a story-telling genre of his own devising, which the author has named "tales within dreams." All four modes maintain a fluid identity; often they merge unpredictably, or abruptly intersect. Unlike previous anthologies, *Second Simplicity* aims to showcase not only the poetry for which Bonnefoy is world renowned, but also—in equal measure—these inventive compositions in prose. Taking a cue from his own example, the book alternates traditional verse with such freer forms, just as the author has done in several important works over the past twenty years: in fact, that symbiotic approach is a hallmark of this latter phase of his writing.

The selection originates—in more ways than one—with poems from *Beginning and End of the Snow* (as I would render the title; though please compare the Select Bibliography). Published in 1991, this verse cycle stands as a watershed in Bonnefoy's oeuvre. From here on, he converts to a plainer and more limpid style, coupled with

a notable shift in imagery: changes that correspond to an autumn and winter sojourn in New England. Given his earlier attachment to the rocky, sun-scoured landscape of Provence—where he spent his summers in the ruined abbey of Valsaintes—perhaps only these radically novel surroundings could have restored his primal state of wonder, that "second simplicity" he has often invoked in his essays. In her letters Emily Dickinson calls her poetry "my snow"—white pages that blow in from nowhere, without warning, and settle in drifts on the table. In his snow poems, Bonnefoy takes up this metaphor and expands it: the snowfall is the emblem of his words, swirling and ephemeral. The two poets are similar in their metaphysical scope; and thematic links naturally arise from their rapt contemplation of the same snowbound landscape. As the crow flies, the "Hopkins Forest" that gives its name to one of Bonnefoy's longer poems is less than eighty miles from Amherst; and the concentrated vision of his shorter pieces often reminds us of Dickinson's compact verses, with their occasional flashes of humor. More than any other single factor, Bonnefoy's frequent walks in the woods near Williamstown suffuse his verse of this period with a rejuvenating light. Or to say it the other way round: these poems wend their way through a new geography, an amplified interior.

Against this all-enveloping backdrop, places other than New England still rise to meet us: above all, Italy and the south of France, those consecrated haunts from Bonnefoy's past. Since his youth, Italian art and architecture have strongly shaped his sensibility. In the ideal, composite city of "The Only Rose," Sangallo's church of San Biagio emerges from snow flurries, in the midst of a dream. And moving further back through memory, under the snows of age the poet rediscovers the Lot Valley meadows of his boyhood, in a temporal fusion that parallels Yeats. As in the "Lake Isle of Innisfree," which Bonnefoy had translated shortly before, here all tenses are conflated into one. In *Beginning and End of the Snow*, winter scenes in America

alternate with visions of summer in Provence, just as age alternates with youth. The book sets a pattern Bonnefoy will continue to follow, up to the present: throughout his later poems, the seasons are constantly superimposed. Time closes its circle, as winter meditates on infancy; and once connected, the entire ring collapses inward, or opens out on timelessness. Summer leaves recall a snowstorm, and snowflakes swarm like bees.

The Wandering Life of 1993—a multilayered work, largely untranslated as yet—is the first of Bonnefoy's collections to interweave poetry and prose. As in the New England cycle, he breaks new ground with his "Impressions at Sunset," verses of an almost Yeatsian diction and rhythm. Though loosely related to some of his essays on painting, this freewheeling sketch diverges from most of his lyric work in both subject and technique; it seems to echo his incomparable translations of the Irish poet into French, completed several years earlier. In other poems, setting aside the snow imagery of the previous book, Bonnefoy returns to the leitmotif of his oeuvre: the immutable presence of stone, which he has called the "abyss of fullness" that "exemplifies the real." In "A Stone," placed strategically at the center of the volume, the poet yearns to inscribe a "circle on the rock," some sign of permanent reality; but in the end he must concede that "the stone closes to our vow." The bleak resistance of rock contrasts sharply with the life-giving waters that both nourish fruit and reflect it in their "saving light."

Often paired, the interlocking themes of water and stone run through Bonnefoy's later work like an ineluctable polarity. The longest verse sequence in *The Wandering Life*, "From Wind and Smoke," develops marine motifs linked to the *Odyssey;* but it also compares Helen to a "great reddish boulder" lifted onto the ramparts of Troy, an impervious object of desire. In other passages, she becomes a stone statue or even a pure illusion "made from wind and smoke," an unrealized figment of the artist's fantasy. Many of Bonnefoy's later poems refer to Odysseus leaving Troy and his divagations on the way to Ithaca. The conquered city represents both a scene of destruction and a point

of departure, though without any assurance of reaching home. In *The Wandering Life*—a title that speaks for itself—"From Wind and Smoke" deploys such Homeric topoi at length, only to culminate in a somber envoi: "These pages are translations. From a tongue / That haunts the memory I have become." The full stop in the first line mimics the French: an impassioned linguist, Bonnefoy stresses the kinship between creative work and translation—though in this coda, they both partake of a tragic hollowness.

Adrift between reminiscence and reverie, "Beckett's Dinghy"—also drawn from *The Wandering Life*—will hold an obvious interest for English-speaking readers, since it intuits the unstated backdrop of one of our finest writers (shared with France): a rugged seascape Bonnefoy associates with Samuel Beckett's oeuvre. Like many of the French poet's excursions in prose, which often perambulate like inner travelogues, this one converts a specific locale—an island off the coast of Ireland—into a mysterious hinterland of the mind. I can vouch for the autobiographical gist of the incident, since I was with Bonnefoy and his daughter in Sligo around the time when it occurred. In the summer of 1987, we had convened at the Yeats International School, and we all met the "ancient mariner" on the wind-raked beach of Rosses Point. A few years later, after Beckett died, Bonnefoy melded the author's legacy with a memory of the fogbound ocean to forge this "tale within a dream." The captain had told us about his murky connections with Yeats; and given the setting near Ben Bulben, the piece pays homage to both Irish masters.

At the end of "Beckett's Dinghy," Bonnefoy ushers in the "intermittent drumming of the rain." In the opening pages of *The Curved Planks*, published in 2001, the theme of rain predominates, with an insistence unheralded in Bonnefoy's verse up till then. In "Rain Falls on the Ravine," he awakens to the "rain of summer mornings"; as though floating in a boat—another recurrent feature of his late work—he observes

Boughs entangled like a dream, stones
With eyes the rapid stream has closed
And that smile in the sand's embrace.

This softening of the harsh stone imagery so pervasive in Bonnefoy by a rain that consoles, cleanses, and renews seems emblematic of the collection as a whole. Even without any direct appearance, its benign influence can still be felt: in one of the poet's most delicate elaborations of the stone motif—"Passer-by, these are words . . ."—the murmurs of the deceased rise from their graves like mist. In French, "pierre" can refer to a tombstone as well as a rock, and for decades Bonnefoy has played on that ambiguity by entitling many of his poems simply "A Stone." Though they allude to half-effaced epitaphs, they also give voice to the dead themselves, whose words often alternate with his own. *The Curved Planks* contains nine superb examples of the genre, all of them included in this anthology.

Among the many fresh departures of Bonnefoy's later period is his journey to the interior, through the remote reaches of his past. "The House Where I Was Born," a verse sequence from *The Curved Planks,* vividly revisits some of the formative moments of his childhood and adolescence. Often they are refracted through the prism of myth, above all that of Ceres and the mocking boy, who churlishly rejects the plentitude of earth (for a full account, see my afterword to the Farrar, Straus edition); but at times he unveils them with disarming directness. While he has touched on similar turning points in his prose works—particularly his spiritual autobiography, *The Hinterland*—such glimpses of his early years have virtually no antecedent in his poetry until then: this makes them all the more moving. But the fact that "the house where he was born" fans out on other landscapes, on dreams and legends, and ultimately on a humanitarian vision of rescuing the shipwrecked, amply proves that Bonnefoy's true habitation is the house of poetry itself.

All the same, even that refuge remains uncertain. The title story of *The Curved Planks* expands the nautical motif of "The House Where I Was Born" even further. A boy without a family implores a ferryman to become his father; like many of Bonnefoy's narratives in which a child takes part, this one assumes the deceptive guise of a fairy tale. Beneath that alluring surface, it swiftly distorts the fable of the Christ child and Saint Christopher, lending it a cataclysmic twist. Unable to offer the boy shelter, the boatman sweeps him away into a maelstrom, where the "curved planks" of the skiff finally give way. Like the ferryman, the boy swims through a "limitless space of clashing currents, of yawning abysses, of stars." Instead of a benign story with a pat ending, Bonnefoy has written a parable of man's irredeemable homelessness—with no savior to come to his aid.

The short prose work *In a Shard of Mirror,* published in 2006 and still untranslated as yet, blends factual reminiscences with a searching interrogation of the nature of memory itself. Along the way, Bonnefoy recalls his encounters with various literary figures, among them Jorge Luis Borges. This kindred spirit, whose oeuvre reveals innumerable parallels to Bonnefoy's poetry, essays, and tales, is deftly depicted in "Three Recollections of Borges." As with *Beginning and End of the Snow,* the New England background of two of these episodes will strike an appealing chord for American readers; and for anyone who's interested in Borges—which means anyone who values great literature —"Three Recollections of Borges" cannot fail to beguile. While the narrative style of *In a Shard of Mirror* is generally less lyrical and elliptical than that of the other prose selections printed here, the book shares a thematic trend with Bonnefoy's late sonnets: these often adopt the paradigm of cultural portraits, much like the sonnets of Borges himself. Both authors cultivate a close-knit intertextuality, manifested here by allusions to numerous writers, and even by the passing appearance of literary friends such as Jorge Guillén or Jean Starobinski. The benevolence and humor with which the French poet observes his Ar-

gentine peer in the realm of letters tells us volumes about them both, and we often have the impression of eavesdropping on their inner as well as outer dialogues.

The Anchor's Long Chain, an extensive collection of verse and prose that appeared in 2008, also awaits a full translation. It derives its title from the keynote poem, "Ales Stenar": in this contemporary ode on a megalithic site in Sweden, Bonnefoy addresses such universal motifs as fraternal solidarity, the passage of time, and our final confrontation with our own transience. In the earlier story, "The Curved Planks," Bonnefoy had engaged in a rethinking of religious myths—one of the constants of his oeuvre. "Naming the Divine," a prose selection from *The Anchor's Long Chain*, examines the self-denying rigors of the austere "negative theology" he has often discussed in his essays. Such works as *De los nombres de Cristo*, by the sixteenth-century Spanish poet Fray Luis de León, celebrate the many names attributed to God; in Bonnefoy's melancholy yet whimsical account, an obsession with never mentioning the deity leads a whole civilization to its ruin. "America," one of his longer tales from the same volume, will possess a special resonance for the English-language public. In a supple narrative, provoked by his stint as a writer-in-residence in California, the author reflects on the dichotomy of Old World and New, without reaching any facile conclusions. Intriguingly, he attributes the beauty of "pure geometrical shapes" to the sunlit parade of American adolescents. But in a letter he wrote me at the time I was translating the story, he commented dryly that "unlike some," he would never discount either side of Western culture. Above all, here he ruminates on the pliant workings of literary invention: its zigzags from confusion to certainty, and back again, and its unforeseen links with childhood, experience, and place.

The anthology almost seems to come full circle with the sprightly poem "The Painter Named Snow," which harks back to the childlike élan and stylistic transparence of *Beginning and End of the Snow*. All the same, in formal terms, this winter scherzo differs decisively from

the more traditional contours of the earlier sequence, wrought with short verses and compact strophes which often recall Dickinson or Frost. Instead, the pithy sentences of "The Painter Named Snow" hover between the prose poem and the broadly spun lines of Whitman or Saint-John Perse. By wryly picturing Adam and Eve in cold-weather togs, Bonnefoy foreshadows two darker works that will bring *The Anchor's Long Chain* to an end; brooding meditations on the expulsion from Eden, they also tap painterly metaphors. In this lighthearted poem, by contrast, the "painter named snow" cheerfully limns—not a paradise lost—but a world regained.

The most striking feature of *The Anchor's Long Chain* is a sonnet cycle, unprecedented in Bonnefoy's work. These lapidary poems reflect his aesthetic maturity, crystallizing themes he has advanced before; but they also demonstrate his youthfulness, his daring impulse to experiment with a verse form some might consider outdated, especially in France. In the United States, several generations of our principal poets, from John Berryman to Marilyn Hacker, have renewed the tradition with emotional clout and coruscating flair. But besides Jacques Réda, most remarkably in his *Sonnets de Dublin*, none of Bonnefoy's leading French contemporaries has cultivated the form; and though a younger writer, Hédi Kaddour, recently embraced it with verve, his incisive snapshots, like Guy Goffette's "thirteen-line sonnets," have even less in common with Bonnefoy's poetic vision than Réda's sonorous lines. We must look to Borges—whom Bonnefoy resembles in so many ways, as I noted before—for the closest analogy. Both come to the sonnet late in life, and both use it to invoke cultural forebears who have haunted their imaginations. Borges commemorates Whitman, Emerson, Spinoza, Heine, Cervantes, and Milton, among others. Bonnefoy erects monuments in verse—in some cases "tombeaux" ("tombs"), reminiscent of Mallarmé's—to Baudelaire, Verlaine, Leopardi, Wordsworth, and Mallarmé himself.

In the poem on Baudelaire, Bonnefoy underscores his belief that the "JGF" to whom the nineteenth-century poet dedicated two of

his texts was actually his mistress, Jeanne Duval—a view he has propounded in one of his essays. As for Mallarmé, he is not only portrayed on his beloved boat ("la fluide yole à jamais littéraire," as Valéry called it), his presence makes itself felt throughout this densely allusive sonnet cycle. For example, Bonnefoy's "Tombeau de Paul Verlaine" cites the "shallow stream" and "cooing dove" from Mallarmé's own sonnet on Verlaine, while his memorial to Leopardi integrates several facets of the "Sonnet en -yx." Naturally, the great Italian's lyric work—which Bonnefoy has translated with lucid empathy—also illumines the poem, much like the moon accompanying Leopardi over the hills. The image accords with one of the latter's favorite motifs: we need only call to mind "Alla luna" or "Il tramonto della luna"; though above all, the sonnet adverts to his lesser-known "Canto notturno di un pastore errante dell'Asia."

While Borges limits himself mainly to portraits of writers, Mallarmé's diverse exercises in the genre—"médaillons" or "hommages," in prose or in verse—pose as early models for both Bonnefoy's *In a Shard of Mirror* and for his sonnets, by depicting painters and composers as well as authors. Although Wordsworth's *The Prelude* will be familiar to most Anglophone readers, some of Bonnefoy's other sources may appear more obscure. "The Invention of the Seven-Pipe Flute" relates to a story by Jules Laforgue, penned when he was in the last stage of tuberculosis and rapidly losing his breath; only a few days later, he died at the age of twenty-seven. "To the Author of 'Night' " paraphrases another gripping tale, this one by Guy de Maupassant; to English-speakers, it will recall the eerie ambience of Poe—a literary touchstone in France, thanks to the translations by Baudelaire and Mallarmé. In a recent note to me, Bonnefoy asserted that the poem's last line also draws on the latter's account of hearing a clock's twelve strokes no longer as the midnight hour, but as the pure sound of timelessness.

In other sonnets, Bonnefoy honors the works of a composer, an artist, and several architects he has long admired: "Abschied" from

Mahler's *Das Lied von der Erde*, three canvases by Poussin, Alberti's "Malatesta Temple" in Rimini, the San Giorgio church by Palladio in Venice, and Sangallo's splendid nave of San Biagio in Montepulciano (previously evoked in *Beginning and End of the Snow*). All the brilliant "medallions" listed above are included in *Second Simplicity*, as well as a few that break the pattern: a sonnet on Ulysses deciding to bypass Ithaca after all, another on an unnamed walker in a rock-strewn landscape (the poet himself, perhaps), and eleven free-style verses on a tree in the rue Descartes—actually a public mural by Pierre Alechinsky, with Bonnefoy's poem inscribed in large letters beside it.

The gnomic aphorisms of "Remarks on the Horizon" oscillate between philosophy and autobiography, poetry and fiction: like many of the prose works in *The Anchor's Long Chain*, they weave a richly nuanced symphony, echoing the author's vast corpus of writings on literature and art. In his recollections of Borges, Bonnefoy had mulled astutely over a tale by Hawthorne, and here he places a key vignette from Melville's years in the Berkshires beside a brief aperçu of Proust's Martinville. Baroque painting—particularly in the manner of Poussin's son-in-law, Gaspard Dughet—provides a backdrop for the sweeping landscape of "Leaving the Garden: A Variant." In this excursus on the story of Adam and Eve, Bonnefoy weighs our attraction to images as opposed to unmediated nature, art as opposed to life; building slowly to a climax, he arrives at some unexpected insights, subtle and open-ended. In "Another Variant," he takes up the biblical legend again in more agonized tones, focusing on the pivotal relationship between language and consciousness. In a familiar sonnet by Borges, the Creation enters fully into being only when Adam gives names to each of its particulars; in Bonnefoy's version of the motif, Eve surpasses her mate in that crucial task. The piece is overshadowed by an early Renaissance painting to which the author has often returned, ever since his youthful sojourn in Florence: Masaccio's searing portrayal of Adam and Eve, mournfully expelled from Paradise. Words remove us from nature as much they enable us to grasp it, Bonnefoy suggests; but

without our fall from innocence, we would be as unaware of love as of suffering and death. Ironically, the distance we gain from immediate reality through poetry and art is what permits us to "found an earth," a world where we can affirm our own mortality.

The anthology nears its close with eight new sonnets by Bonnefoy from the collection *Crossing Out and In*, published in 2010. As he explains in his preface to the book, the "crossing out" of words which wouldn't fit the exacting schema of the sonnet form obliged him to penetrate to a deeper verbal level. Appropriately enough, for his advanced stage in life, he explores the ravages inflicted on us by time in a pair of poems about discolored photographs; and in another, he concludes that in the end, "death says no to all our metaphors." A miniature trilogy, the three sonnets of "The Lost Name" bind labile tropes to a wrenched versification, in keeping with the aesthetic defeat they adumbrate. Brittle and poignant, they might be construed as a self-written epitaph—but this would be a glaring blunder: on the contrary, their stark originality proclaims Bonnefoy's unabated vigor. If the grand "name that devours the book" has been lost, the humbler name of Proust's housekeeper Céleste still shines out, "luminous and round," with its sky-bright overtones intact. And in the twin sonnets of "The Pianist," rejoining Rimbaud's ambition to "changer la vie"—to transform life itself through the potency of words—Bonnefoy lays claim to an ars poetica that denies the constraints of age, paving the way for further voyages of discovery, whether toward darkness or toward light. Bidding the weary musician to leave the house where he has plied the same keyboard day after day, the poet exhorts him: "Open the door and go out. Not knowing / If this is day that breaks, or night that falls."

The last section affixes a lively colophon to the foregoing pages of Bonnefoy's verse and prose. As the author and I were putting the final touches on *Second Simplicity*, he kindly sent me these just-minted works, which he was still revising: they were published in France only a short time ago. It would be hard to conceive a more suitable ending

than these two pairs of variants, each of which sums up broad currents in Bonnefoy's lifework.

In the first diptych, Bonnefoy expresses his nostalgia for vanished civilizations, a theme spun out in almost all his books, from *The Improbable* of 1959 to *The Anchor's Long Chain* of 2008. While most often the cultures he interrogates have existed historically—ancient Greece in "From Wind and Smoke," or medieval Sweden in "Ales Stenar," to cite examples from the present anthology—in his latter phase he has sometimes molded them wholly from his own sensibility. This trend came to the fore in 1988 with *Another Era of Writing*, and it is equally manifest in "Naming the Divine," the disquieting tale of religious purism reprinted in *Second Simplicity*. Like those antecedents, "Voice Heard near a Temple" and "Scared Animal" portray the spectral persistence of the dead. But now their survival has been further magnified, even concretized: no longer merely sensed through their artistic legacies (or their sly young descendants), they themselves call out plaintively, still inhabiting their own terrain. In the first episode, the former worshippers at a ruined shrine seem to haunt it as a disembodied cry; in the second, their enduring spirit has permeated nature itself. The enigmatic creature encountered on the path is but one of their many guises, and their sentience tinges the very moonlight that laves a sacrificial stone.

A message from a sunken collectivity, the furtive animal is above all a figure of speech; like Adam and Eve in "Another Variant," the walkers who capture the beast want to name it. "A weasel, a whale, Hamlet said"—with those quizzical words from act III, scene 2 of the play, Bonnefoy stakes out the ground he really means to plumb in his fictive archaeology: the unearthing of the world through language, which restores to mankind "what is past, and passing, and to come." More than the abandoned temples of religion, he implies, literature conveys an inkling of eternity. In the works of an author like Shakespeare, an age long defunct is both preserved and subsumed as it moves with us through time, both enshrined and universalized. Paradoxically, the

most archaic traits of such texts often anticipate the future. All the same, we will always confront in them distortion, incomprehension, and loss; like the recorder in *Hamlet*, art in its totality is an instrument no single person—and no single people—can fully play.

These tongue-in-cheek allusions also furnish an unexpected bridge to the final works in this volume. The two fantasias on *Hamlet*—each a succinct tour de force—vividly remind us of Bonnefoy's profound closeness to Shakespeare; with radiant precision, he has translated all the lyric poems, as well as a dozen of the plays. *Hamlet* was among the earliest in the series, which dates back all the way to 1957. Apostolically speaking, this is only logical: the Prince of Denmark captivated Mallarmé as well, who composed a curious review of a performance in Paris, similar in shading to Bonnefoy's versions of the theme. Over the decades, the translator's commitment to English letters has branched out into other oeuvres, such as those of Yeats, Keats, and Donne; but Shakespeare has always remained paramount to his thought, about life in general as much as literature. Tellingly, he has devoted a hefty tome of essays to his work—more critical attention than he has bestowed on any other writer, even his much-revered forerunners in the French tradition, such as Baudelaire, Rimbaud, or Mallarmé.

"First Sketch for a Staging of *Hamlet*" proposes an impossible stage-set, in a theater as vast and diffuse as a mountainside, which mirrors the boundlessness of the ideal reader's mind. In "Voice Heard near a Temple," Bonnefoy had quoted from the scene where Hamlet presents his devastating "pièce à clef" at court. As Shakespeare often expostulates, through personae as diverse as Macbeth and Puck, every play is a play within a play: the one that unfurls in the human imagination, to its anguish or delight. But in *Hamlet* the device occupies a place of choice, as the only drama in which the title character himself mounts a skit about a deadly serious theme, and personally directs the actors as Shakespeare must have done. It's no accident that Hamlet, of all the author's inventions, is the one who's most obsessed with "words,

words, words." Of course, Shakespeare was also a thespian for much of his career; but as Borges stresses in "Everything and Nothing," he was actually the main protagonist of all his creations, just like every great writer. The principle overarches all our cultural frontiers—"the stones of time, the voices of space"—which is why Basho turns up on the road to comfort a weeping child: for Bonnefoy, compassion always infuses "the deep heart's core" of literature. He could be speaking of his own lifework when he ends the piece with Shakespeare assuming the central role. "He keeps drawing closer, though we don't know exactly where he is. Maybe he's going to appear at some point on the enormous stage, a hurricane-lamp in his hands: and the mask on his face will be the words of poetry."

Wrongly understood, such a denouement might portend the loveless solipsism Bonnefoy has always abjured, as one of the most pernicious temptations of art. After all, Hamlet is veering here toward a tryst with Ophelia, whose affection he has rejected out of allegiance to his father. But the crux of the matter is: he now intends to rejoin her. Any misprision on this score is clearly belied by the second variation. In "*Hamlet* in the Mountains," the scenario balloons to the verge of dissolution; not just a mountainside, the theater swells to an entire sierra, with no limits in sight. The spectators stream through the landscape by the thousands, and before long they themselves turn into actors, who embody the various roles. There are so many Hamlets and Ophelias, and so many incarnations of the other personae, that the players soon relapse into individuals instead of characters. Or in other words, "all the world's a stage," and literature becomes synonymous with life. We are close here to what Stevens termed the "major reality," in which poetry and nature respond to each other antiphonally, modulating into an interdependent whole. As in the previous diptych about the prolongation of consciousness, this "supreme fiction" brooks no distinction between the living and the dead. At its climax, the ghost of Hamlet's father rides into the multitude, and his red scarf—as always in Bonnefoy, a symbol of remembered love—wafts triumphantly up to the

stars. On one level, he is the author; but on a higher plane, he is everyman, perpetually expressed by language. Through the unifying force of words, and the intrinsic bond among us they foster, the primum mobile of the human drama impels the action forward. In this sense and no other, "l'amor che move il sole e l'altre stelle" affirms our posthumous vitality, without any need of a beyond.

Bonnefoy's fundamental identity with Shakespeare also affords some clues to defining his late manner as a whole. Such a phenomenon often emerges in authors whose longevity permits them to amplify and refine their oeuvre in the seventh, eighth, or even ninth decades of their lives. In the twentieth century, Yeats might stand as the exemplar; and after Shakespeare, Yeats is the poet whom Bonnefoy has translated most prolifically. Undoubtedly, his sonnets on old age reflect the perplexity we often find in the Irish poet's final verse—though they are exempt from his towering rage. Far removed from bitterness, Bonnefoy's late work breathes that calm acceptance which Santayana called "an orchestration of transcended sorrows." Long gone is the surrealist vehemence of his early phase, in which rabid insects devoured the female prototype Douve, and windowpanes were spattered with her blood. Even the pungent regret of his middle years, which followed on the loss of his retreat at Valsaintes in Provence, has steadily ebbed. If themes of aridity and stoniness pervaded both those periods, Bonnefoy's late writing is imbued with a sense of release, evinced by flowing, drifting, or falling water: streams, rivers, oceans, fogs, drizzles, rains, and snow.

Perhaps it's only an American perspective, but I would consider New England in wintertime the "primal scene" of Bonnefoy's past two decades. This is the landscape that inspired *Beginning and End of the Snow*, the collection of 1991 in which his late poetics first announced itself, and winter is the season we instinctively associate with old age. Not only Dickinson, Hawthorne, and Melville but also Frost and Thoreau, with their emphasis on natural simplification and the cli-

matic cycle, seem to have informed Bonnefoy's attraction to the region; and as his recollections show, he was impressed by its appeal to Borges as well, a subliminal reinforcement. I would posit that its quiet woods and fields, rustic and unadorned, initially gave shape to his pared-down aesthetic of these recent years. The sheet of fallen snow, shining blankly from his windowsill to the horizon, lay before him like an unwritten page.

The final works of some authors, like James Joyce or Ezra Pound, abound in willful complexities that some readers may find obscure; by contrast, Bonnefoy's writing has evolved toward a "second simplicity" of imagery and diction. He has whittled his tropes and phrases in order to arrive at the sheer essence of each text. This quality is the opposite of simplemindedness: what has come "second" is a distillation of the many decades of rigorous thought that have gone before. Nor should it be mistaken for an endgame, but rather an inmost path among those labyrinthine byways of the intellect which he is still exploring in his critical studies—most recently on such diverse topics as the "black paintings" of Goya or the musicality of verse. Over his immense trajectory, after scaling the most arduous slopes of philosophy, literature, history, and art, Bonnefoy has attained a luminous plateau, not unlike the light-washed settings so frequent in this latest chapter of his work. While lengthening shadows sometimes overtake that clarity, they only throw his hard-won peace into even keener relief.

Again, it may be merely an English-speaker's point of view, but I would infer that Bonnefoy's engagement with poetry in our language has engendered another facet of his late manner, the gradual approximation of his French to the rhythms of English verse. In section IX of "The House Where I Was Born," he even goes so far as to insert some original lines of Keats directly into his own: tellingly, they harmonize without a hitch, despite the surface disparity. In fact, the poet's assimilation of our language often assists Anglophone translators of his work, just as it does in the case of Borges. Repeatedly, Bonnefoy has voiced his attachment to the iamb, the characteristic metrical foot of

our poetry. In another poem from *The Curved Planks*, not reprinted here, he praises the basic rhythm most of us take for granted, hearing it anew as only a foreigner could:

> Two syllables, a short and then a long:
> The iamb hesitates, but also yearns
> To leap beyond the breath that merely hopes
> And enter into all that meaning gives.

Given his many decades of praxis in the art of translation—not only of Shakespeare but of Donne, Keats, and Yeats—it should hardly surprise us that Bonnefoy's prosody often transposes iambic tetrameter or pentameter, despite the resistance of French to marked patterns of stress. Renditions of his verse into English must strive to detect that faintly audible heartbeat in his poems, and make it sound forth.

Admittedly, this characteristic also relates to an individual trait: anyone who has heard Bonnefoy read aloud will have noted the unusual gravity of his inflections and cadences in French. Even so, pursuing this thread somewhat further, we might maintain that there is a certain succession of English imprints on his verse in these past two decades. In the nineties, Dickinson and Yeats come to the fore; but in the current phase, Shakespeare predominates—Shakespeare at his most transparent, as in sonnets 18, 31, or 73. In Bonnefoy's latest poems, the sonnet form itself instills a certain serenity, which almost allows the words to write themselves, without recourse to drastic metaphors or tortured syntax. In the preface to *Crossing Out and In*, a collection made up entirely of sonnets, and just completed in 2010, he elucidates: "Words, words as such, their own aural reality authorized by this primacy of form, have established links among themselves I never suspected." Here authorship modestly submits to a process of elimination—though as we know, "ars est celare artem." Revealingly, Bonnefoy's increasing recourse to the sonnet in his latter years parallels a cumulative project: his integral translation of Shakespeare's sonnets.

Though the sonnets are clearly relevant to Bonnefoy's poetry, it might be contended that Shakespeare's plays have marked his late aesthetic on the broadest scale. As I stated at the outset, this anthology mimes Bonnefoy's own procedure in several of his recent books, by blending traditional verse with more fluid genres, including a gamut of lyrical prose—sometimes as sustained as the "tales within dreams," which straddle fiction and poetry. Once again, his affinity with Borges may have spurred him to forge some of these iridescent alloys. But in framing the architecture of his works—with the possible exception of *El hacedor*, since the *Antología personal* belongs to another order—Borges never systematically meshed prose and verse to the extent that Bonnefoy has done, nor did he develop nearly as many hybrids. To this reader at least, such a panoply of varying tones, styles, polymorphs, and crosscurrents within a single work suggests a fertile provenance: the dramas of Shakespeare. With fascination and infinite care, Bonnefoy has translated them into French like no one before him; and translation is an art he has described as striking inward over time, especially if the translator is a writer himself.

Reverting to the elusive domain of attitude, what most consistently underpins Bonnefoy's late stance is a tranquil fearlessness—a trust in continuous renewal, though without any clinging to the self. In one of the "Stones," in a point and counterpoint to their funerary theme, he concludes:

> Still this night is bright,
> As we desired our death might be.
> It whitens the trees, they expand.
> Their foliage: sand, then foam.
> Day is breaking, even beyond time.

Bonnefoy greets his finitude imperturbably, with a grace that almost seems preternatural; but when time folds back on itself as here, ending and beginning are the same. Significantly—and in contrast to most

writers in their latter years—Bonnefoy has focused on children as the most prevalent observers and actors in his oeuvre of the past two decades, though they were virtually absent from it before. Pensively or genially, they range throughout his recent works with their naive questioning and wide-eyed games, as though the poet were reliving his earliest youth. Congregating in groups, as in "America" or "Naming the Divine," they may take on a somewhat sinister slant; but when he meets them alone, the tone usually shifts to a warm and intimate key. Archetypal but never abstract, these recurrent companions may best be understood as emblems of poetic awareness, surveying the world with a candid, undaunted gaze.

In Shakespeare's romances, such authorial alter egos loom in and out with similar insistence, though they wear the trappings of age. I am thinking of Time as well as Paulina in *The Winter's Tale*; the Apparitions and Belarius in *Cymbeline*; or Gower, the wraith from the ashes who "narrates" *Pericles*. Like the sonnets—and like Bonnefoy's current phase of writing—these final dramas demonstrate that memory, sustained by the vivifying force of human speech, is the only form of resurrection. At the beginning of *The Tempest*, Prospero enjoins Miranda to recover the past, the "dark backward and abysm of time." At the end, after ruling the winds and waves through his spells, he discards them so that ordinary life can resume its course. Set in motion by forgiveness, a return to the everyday world signals the culmination of Shakespeare's art—though with a deeper consciousness than before, a "second simplicity." In Bonnefoy's late work, with the immediacy of a child, the author deliberately drops "the mask of poetry." When the "omnipresent director" has stretched his craft to its ultimate reach, the "greatest scene of all" overflows the bounds of the text, and the play becomes the real.

Hoyt Rogers

FROM DÉBUT ET FIN DE LA NEIGE

BEGINNING AND END OF THE SNOW

« PREMIÈRE NEIGE … »

Première neige tôt ce matin. L'ocre, le vert
Se réfugient sous les arbres.

Seconde, vers midi. Ne demeure
De la couleur
Que les aiguilles de pins
Qui tombent elles aussi plus dru parfois que la neige.

Puis, vers le soir,
Le fléau de la lumière s'immobilise.
Les ombres et les rêves ont même poids.

Un peu de vent
Écrit du bout du pied un mot hors du monde.

"FIRST SNOWFALL . . ."

First snowfall, early this morning. Ochre and green
Take refuge under the trees.

The second batch, toward noon. No color's left
But the needles shed by pines,
Falling even thicker than the snow.

Then, toward evening,
Light's scale comes to rest.
Shadows and dreams weigh the same.

With a toe, a puff of wind
Writes a word outside the world.

LE MIROIR

Hier encore
Les nuages passaient
Au fond noir de la chambre.
Mais à présent le miroir est vide.

Neiger
Se désenchevêtre du ciel.

THE MIRROR

Yesterday
Clouds still drifted
In the room's black depths.
But now the mirror is empty.

Snowing
Unravels from the sky.

LA CHARRUE

Cinq heures. La neige encore. J'entends des voix
À l'avant du monde.

Une charrue
Comme une lune au troisième quartier
Brille, mais la recouvre
La nuit d'un pli de la neige.

Et cet enfant
A toute la maison pour lui, désormais. Il va
D'une fenêtre à l'autre. Il presse
Ses doigts contre la vitre. Il voit
Des gouttes se former là où il cesse
D'en pousser la buée vers le ciel qui tombe.

THE PLOW

Five o'clock. More snow. I hear voices
Ahead, at the prow of the world.

A plow
Glints like a three-quarter moon,
But a fold of snow
Wraps it in night.

From now on, this child
Has the house to himself. He goes
From window to window. He sticks
His fingers against the glass. He sees
Droplets bead where he stops
Nudging steam toward a falling sky.

LE PEU D'EAU

À ce flocon
Qui sur ma main se pose, j'ai désir
D'assurer l'éternel
En faisant de ma vie, de ma chaleur,
De mon passé, de ces jours d'à présent,
Un instant simplement : cet instant-ci, sans bornes.

Mais déjà il n'est plus
Qu'un peu d'eau, qui se perd
Dans la brume des corps qui vont dans la neige.

A BIT OF WATER

I long to grant eternity
To this flake
That alights on my hand,
By making my life, my warmth,
My past, my present days
Into a moment: the boundless
Moment of now.

But already it's no more
Than a bit of water, lost in the fog
Of bodies moving through snow.

LE JARDIN

Il neige.
Sous les flocons la porte
Ouvre enfin au jardin
De plus que le monde.

J'avance. Mais se prend
Mon écharpe à du fer
Rouillé, et se déchire
En moi l'étoffe du songe.

THE GARDEN

It's snowing.
Under the flakes, a door opens at last
On the garden beyond the world.

I set out. But my scarf
Snags on a rusty nail,
And the cloth of my dreams is torn.

L'ÉTÉ ENCORE

J'avance dans la neige, j'ai fermé
Les yeux, mais la lumière sait franchir
Les paupières poreuses, et je perçois
Que dans mes mots c'est encore la neige
Qui tourbillonne, se resserre, se déchire.

Neige,
Lettre que l'on retrouve et que l'on déplie,
Et l'encre en a blanchi et dans les signes
La gaucherie de l'esprit est visible
Qui ne sait qu'en enchevêtrer les ombres claires.

Et on essaye de lire, on ne comprend pas
Qui s'intéresse à nous dans la mémoire,
Sinon que c'est l'été encore ; et que l'on voit
Sous les flocons les feuilles, et la chaleur
Monter du sol absent comme une brume.

SUMMER AGAIN

I walk on, through the snow. I've closed
My eyes, but the light knows how to breach
My porous lids. And I perceive
That in my words it's still the snow
That eddies, thickens, shears apart.

Snow,
Letter we find again and unfold:
The ink has paled, and the bleached-out marks
Betray an awkwardness of mind
That makes their lucid shadows just a muddle.

We try to read, but we can't grasp who this is
In our memory who's taking such an interest
In ourselves, except it's still summer; and we see
The leaves behind the snowflakes, where the heat
Still rises from the absent ground like mist.

« ON DIRAIT … »

On dirait beaucoup d'e muets dans une phrase.
On sent qu'on ne leur doit
Que des ombres de métaphores.

On dirait,
Dès qu'il neige plus dru,
De ces mains qui refusent d'autres mains

Mais jouent avec les doigts qu'elles refusent.

"IT'S LIKE . . ."

It's like a phrase with lots of mute *e*'s.
You feel you only owe them
Shadows of metaphors.

When the snow falls thicker,
It's like
Hands pushing other hands away

But playing with the fingers they refuse.

NOLI ME TANGERE

Hésite le flocon dans le ciel bleu
À nouveau, le dernier flocon de la grande neige.

Et c'est comme entrerait au jardin celle qui
Avait bien dû rêver ce qui pourrait être,
Ce regard, ce dieu simple, sans souvenir
Du tombeau, sans pensée que le bonheur,
Sans avenir
Que sa dissipation dans le bleu du monde.

« Non, ne me touche pas », lui dirait-il,
Mais même dire non serait de lumière.

NOLI ME TANGERE

A snowflake wavers in the sky, blue
Again—the big snowfall's final flake.

As though she entered the garden,
Having dreamed of what she'd find:
This gaze, this simple god, not remembering
The tomb—no thought but happiness,
No future
But to merge with the blueness of the world.

"No, don't touch me," he'd say;
But even his saying no
Would be made of light.

« JUSTE AVANT L'AUBE … »

Juste avant l'aube
Je regarde à travers les vitres, et je crois comprendre
Qu'il a cessé de neiger. Une flaque bleue
S'étend, brillante un peu, devant les arbres,
D'une paroi à l'autre de la nuit.

Je sors.
Je descends précautionneusement l'escalier de bois
Dont les marches sont nivelées par la neige fraîche.
Le froid cerne et pénètre mes chevilles,
Il semble que l'esprit en soit plus clair,
Qui perçoit mieux le silence des choses.

Dort-il encore
Dans l'enchevêtrement du tas de bois
Serré sous la fenêtre,
Le chipmunk, notre voisin simple,
Ou est-il déjà à errer dans les crissements et le froid ?
Je vois d'infimes marques devant la porte.

"JUST BEFORE DAWN . . ."

Just before dawn
I look through the window: the snow
Must have stopped. A swath of blue,
Gleaming in front of the trees,
Laps at the walls of night.

I go outside,
Picking my way down the wooden steps,
Caked high with the new-fallen snow.
My ankles are ringed by the piercing chill;
It seems to clarify the mind,
Which starts to hear the silence of things.

I wonder if the chipmunk,
Our simple neighbor, is still asleep—
Or has he already left
The tangled woodpile by the sill
To rove through the crackling cold?
I notice tiny tracks before the door.

LES FLAMBEAUX

Neige
Qui as cessé de donner, qui n'es plus
Celle qui vient mais celle qui attend
En silence, ayant apporté mais sans qu'encore
On ait pris, et pourtant, toute la nuit,
Nous avons aperçu, dans l'embuement
Des vitres parfois même ruisselantes,
Ton étincellement sur la grande table.

Neige, notre chemin,
Immaculé encore, pour aller prendre
Sous les branches courbées et comme attentives
Ces flambeaux, ce qui est, qui ont paru
Un à un, et brûlé, mais semblent s'éteindre
Comme aux yeux du désir quand il accède
Aux biens dont il rêvait (car c'est souvent
Quand tout se dénouerait peut-être, que s'efface
En nous de salle en salle le reflet
Du ciel, dan les miroirs), ô neige, touche

Encore ces flambeaux, renflamme-les
Dans le froid de cette aube ; et qu'à l'exemple
De tes flocons qui déjà les assaillent
De leur insouciance, feu plus clair,
Et malgré tant de fièvre dans la parole
Et tant de nostalgie dans le souvenir,

THE TORCHES

Snow
You've stopped giving,
Stopped arriving:
Now you wait in silence with your gift.
We don't accept it yet. But through the night,
Through the windows that dripped with mist,
We sensed your sheen
Along the vast tabletop.

Snow, still immaculate, our path
To all that is: we take these torches
From limbs that are bowed down
As though expectantly.
One by one, their flames have flared and died,
Just as when desire achieves its dreams. (Often,
At the turning point when all might come aright,
The sky's reflection ebbs from our mirrors,
Room by room.) Snow, touch

These torches again, light them
In the chill of this dawn. Your flurries
Already storm them with their brighter,
Carefree fire. Despite the longing in our memory,
And fever in our speech, our words

Nos mots ne cherchent plus les autres mots mais les avoisinent,
Passent auprès d'eux, simplement,
Et si l'un en a frôlé un, et s'ils s'unissent,
Ce ne sera qu'encore ta lumière,
Notre brièveté qui se dissémine,
L'écriture qui se dissipe, sa tâche faite.

(Et tel flocon s'attarde, on le suit des yeux,
On aimerait le regarder toujours,
Tel autre s'est posé sur la main offerte.

Et tel plus lent et comme égaré s'éloigne
Et tournoie, puis revient. Et n'est-ce dire
Qu'un mot, un autre mot encore, à inventer,
Rédimerait le monde ? Mais on ne sait
Si on entend ce mot ou si on le rêve.)

Should move as snowflakes move:
Not seeking other words,
But only drawing near them, passing by.
And if one should brush another, so they join,
Your light will still sow our briefness—
Scattering what we've written, once the task is done.

(My eyes follow a snowflake where it dawdles;
I could look at it forever.
Another one alights on the palm of my hand.

A slower flake seems lost: it wanders off,
Spins around, and then comes back. Do we mean
A word, another word we might invent,
Could redeem the world? But we don't know
If we hear this word, or only dream it.)

HOPKINS FOREST

J'étais sorti
Prendre de l'eau au puits, auprès des arbres,
Et je fus en présence d'un autre ciel.
Disparues les constellations d'il y a un instant encore,
Les trois quarts du firmament étaient vides,
Le noir le plus intense y régnait seul,
Mais à gauche, au-dessus de l'horizon,
Mêlé à la cime des chênes,
Il y avait un amas d'étoiles rougeoyantes
Comme un brasier, d'où montait même une fumée.

Je rentrai
Et je rouvris le livre sur la table.
Page après page,
Ce n'étaient que des signes indéchiffrables,
Des agrégats de formes d'aucun sens
Bien que vaguement récurrentes,
Et par-dessous une blancheur d'abîme
Comme si ce qu'on nomme l'esprit tombait là, sans bruit,
Comme une neige.
Je tournai cependant les pages.

Bien des années plus tôt,
Dans un train au moment où le jour se lève
Entre Princeton Junction et Newark,
C'est-à-dire deux lieux de hasard pour moi,

HOPKINS FOREST

I had gone out
To draw water from the well, down by the trees:
And now I stood in the presence of another sky.
The constellations of a moment past had fled.
The firmament was three-quarters blank,
And here deepest black reigned alone.
But to the left, on the horizon,
Mingled with a canopy of oaks,
Reddish stars clustered
Like a bonfire, even trailing smoke.

I went back inside;
I opened the book
On the table again. Page after page,
Symbols I couldn't decipher:
Shapes lumped together, vaguely serial,
But meaningless. And underneath,
A white abyss,
As if the something we call spirit
Were falling . . . noiseless as snow.
I turned the pages anyway.

Many years before, at daybreak on a train
Between Princeton Junction and Newark—
For me, two places picked from a hat,

Deux retombées des flèches de nulle part,
Les voyageurs lisaient, silencieux
Dans la neige qui balayait les vitres grises,
Et soudain,
Dans un journal ouvert à deux pas de moi,
Une grande photographie de Baudelaire,
Toute une page
Comme le ciel se vide à la fin du monde
Pour consentir au désordre des mots.

J'ai rapproché ce rêve et ce souvenir
Quand j'ai marché, d'abord tout un automne
Dans des bois où bientôt ce fut la neige
Qui triompha, dans beaucoup de ces signes
Que l'on reçoit, contradictoirement,
Du monde dévasté par le langage.
Prenait fin le conflit de deux principes,
Me semblait-il, se mêlaient deux lumières,
Se refermaient les lèvres de la plaie.
La masse blanche du froid tombait par rafales
Sur la couleur, mais un toit au loin, une planche
Peinte, restée debout contre une grille,
C'était encore la couleur, et mystérieuse
Comme un qui sortirait du sépulcre et, riant :
« Non, ne me touche pas », dirait-il au monde.

Two arrows ricocheted from nowhere.
The travelers went on reading,
Silent as the snow
That swept the gray windows.
And next to me, suddenly,
In a newspaper someone unfolded:
Baudelaire. A huge photograph,
An entire page, like the sky that empties
When the world comes to an end,
Consenting to the disarray of words.

I set that dream beside that memory
While walking in the woods, all autumn at first.
But soon the snow had triumphed there,
In many of the signs we glean—by an apparent
Contradiction—from a world
Language has laid waste.
It seemed the war of those two principles
Was winding down; it seemed
Their double radiance was fusing now:
That the lips of the wound would close.
Driving gusts buried every hue beneath a cold
Mass of white. But on a distant roof,
Or painted board propped against a fence,
Here and there a color still appeared: mysterious
As one who issues from a sepulcher
And tells us blithely, "Touch me not."

Je dois vraiment beaucoup à Hopkins Forest,
Je la garde à mon horizon, dans sa partie
Qui quitte le visible pour l'invisible
Par le tressaillement du bleu des lointains.
Je l'écoute, à travers les bruits, et parfois même,
L'été, poussant du pied les feuilles mortes
D'autres années, claires dans la pénombre
Des chênes trop serrés parmi les pierres,
Je m'arrête, je crois que ce sol s'ouvre
À l'infini, que ces feuilles y tombent
Sans hâte, ou bien remontent, le haut, le bas
N'étant plus, ni le bruit, sauf le léger
Chuchotement des flocons qui bientôt
Se multiplient, se rapprochent, se nouent
—Et je revois alors tout l'autre ciel,
J'entre pour un instant dans la grande neige.

I truly owe a lot to Hopkins Forest.
On my horizon, I keep it where the seen
Retreats to the unseen, trembling
In the final depths of blue.
I listen to its sounds through other sounds.
Sometimes, in summer, my feet
Nudge dead leaves from former years,
Pale in the shade of oaks
Grown too thick among the rocks . . .
I stop. The ground seems to open
On infinity. The leaves are slowly
Falling there, or rising up and down:
No difference now, no rustle but the light
Whisper of flakes that swarm and weave
Until they bind. And then I see the other sky again;
I enter the whirling snow.

LA SEULE ROSE

I

Il neige, c'est revenir dans une ville
Où, et je le découvre en avançant
Au hasard dans des rues qui toutes sont vides,
J'aurais vécu heureux une autre enfance.
Sous les flocons j'aperçois des façades
Qui ont beauté plus que rien de ce monde.
Seuls parmi nous Alberti puis Sangallo
À San Biagio, dans la salle la plus intense
Qu'ait bâtie le désir, ont approché
De cette perfection, de cette absence.

Et je regarde donc, avidement,
Ces masses que la neige me dérobe.
Je recherche surtout, dans la blancheur
Errante, ces frontons que je vois qui montent
À un plus haut niveau de l'apparence.
Ils déchirent la brume, c'est comme si
D'une main délivrée de la pesanteur
L'architecte d'ici avait fait vivre
D'un seul grand trait floral
La forme que voulait de siècle en siècle
La douleur d'être né dans la matière.

THE ONLY ROSE

I

It's snowing: and so I've returned to the city
Where I might have lived another childhood,
Happily. I discover this, walking at random
Along the streets, all of them deserted.
Through snowflakes, I catch sight of facades
Whose beauty has no equal in this world.
Alberti, then Sangallo at San Biagio,
In the loftiest, the most intense of rooms
That longing ever built: among us, only they
Come close to this perfection, to this absence.

And I keep peering, avidly, at masses
That the snow halfway conceals.
Above the roving whiteness, I seek out
The pediments, and see them rise
To higher ranges of the visible.
They rend the mist, as though their earthly
Architect had fathered forth in stone
The centuries' desire, the final form
Of birth into the suffering of matter—
And then, with a single stroke, had freed it
Into weightlessness, and tossed it
Like a flower from his hand.

II

Et là-haut je ne sais si c'est la vie
Encore, ou la joie seule, qui se détache
Sur ce ciel qui n'est plus de notre monde.
Ô bâtisseurs
Non tant d'un lieu que d'un regain de l'espérance,
Qu'y a-t-il au secret de ces parois
Qui devant moi s'écartent ? Ce que je vois
Le long des murs, ce sont des niches vides,
Des pleins et des déliés, d'où s'évapore
Par la grâce des nombres
Le poids de la naissance dans l'exil,
Mais de la neige s'y est mise et s'y entasse,
Je m'approche de l'une d'elles, la plus basse,
Je fais tomber un peu de sa lumière,
Et soudain c'est le pré de mes dix ans,
Les abeilles bourdonnent,
Ce que j'ai dans mes mains, ces fleurs, ces ombres,
Est-ce presque du miel, est-ce de la neige ?

III

J'avance alors, jusque sous l'arche d'une porte.
Les flocons tourbillonnent, effaçant
La limite entre le dehors et cette salle
Où des lampes sont allumées : mais elles-mêmes
Une sorte de neige, qui hésite
Entre le haut, le bas, dans cette nuit.
C'est comme si j'étais sur un second seuil.

II

Up there, I couldn't say if this
Is life anymore, or joy alone, framed by a sky
That no longer belongs to our world.
O builders
Not of a place but of hope regained,
What is the secret of these walls
That open up before me? I see
Along their sides the vacant niches,
The slim or thicker lines
Where your numbers intercede, to write away
The burden of our exile into birth.
But snow piles up in their hollows;
Edging close to the lowest shelf,
I topple a bit of its light.
And suddenly, here's the meadow
When I was ten, buzzing with bees:
And in my hands—are these flowers now,
Or shadows? Honey almost, or snow?

III

I move forward, under the archway of a door.
Snowflakes whirl, blurring the line
Between the outside and the inside of this room
Where lamps are lit—themselves
A kind of snow, flickering
High or low amid this night:
As though I'd reached another threshold.

Et au-delà ce même bruit d'abeilles
Dans le bruit de la neige. Ce que disaient
Les abeilles sans nombre de l'été,
Semble le refléter l'infini des lampes.

Et je voudrais
Courir, comme du temps de l'abeille, cherchant
Du pied la balle souple, car peut-être
Je dors, et rêve, et vais par les chemins d'enfance.

IV

Mais ce que je regarde, c'est de la neige
Durcie, qui s'est glissée sur le dallage
Et s'accumule aux bases des colonnes
À gauche, à droite, et loin devant dans la pénombre.
Absurdement je n'ai d'yeux que pour l'arc
Que cette boue dessine sur la pierre.
J'attache ma pensée à ce qui n'a
Pas de nom, pas de sens. Ô mes amis,
Alberti, Brunelleschi, Sangallo,
Palladio qui fais signe de l'autre rive,
Je ne vous trahis pas, cependant, j'avance,
La forme la plus pure reste celle
Qu'a pénétrée la brume qui s'efface,
La neige piétinée est la seule rose.

And beyond it is that same humming of bees
In the sound of the snow. What they said,
The unnumbered bees of summer, seems
Reflected by the lamps, and without end.

And how I'd love to run,
As in the bee-loud days, kicking
The pliant ball; for it may be
That I'm sleeping now, and dreaming, and following
Those childhood paths.

IV

But what I'm looking at is hardened snow
That's crept across the flagstones,
Clumping at the base of columns, right
And left, and on into the dimness far ahead.
Absurdly, I'm led forward by the arc
This mud has inscribed on the stone.
I fix my thoughts on what's bereft
Of any meaning, any name. O my friends,
Alberti, Brunelleschi, Sangallo—
Palladio who beckons from the other shore—
I do not betray you: all the same, I move forward.
The purest form is still the shape
That mist inhabits, and dissolves.
Trampled snow is the only rose.

FROM LA VIE ERRANTE

THE WANDERING LIFE

IMPRESSIONS, SOLEIL COUCHANT

Le peintre qu'on nomme l'orage a bien travaillé, ce soir,
Des figures de grande beauté sont assemblées
Sous un porche à gauche du ciel, là où se perdent
Ces marches phosphorescentes dans la mer.
Et il y a de l'agitation dans cette foule,
C'est comme si un dieu avait paru,
Visage d'or parmi nombre d'autres sombres.

Mais ces cris de surprise, presque ces chants,
Ces musiques de fifres et ces rires
Ne nous viennent pas de ces êtres mais de leur forme.
Les bras qui s'ouvrent se rompent, se multiplient,
Les gestes se dilatent, se diluent,
Sans cesse la couleur devient autre couleur
Et autre chose que la couleur, ainsi des îles,
Des bribes de grandes orgues dans la nuée.
Si c'est là la résurrection des morts, celle-ci ressemble
À la crête des vagues à l'instant où elles se brisent,
Et maintenant le ciel est presque vide,
Rien qu'une masse rouge qui se déplace
Vers un drap d'oiseaux noirs, au nord, piaillant, la nuit.

Ici ou là
Une flaque encore, trouée
Par un brandon de la beauté en cendres.

IMPRESSIONS AT SUNSET

This evening, the painter they call a storm
Has done good work: exquisite figures
Gather to the left beneath a portico
Of sky, where phosphorescent stairs
Drop down to the sea. And in this throng
There is a stir, as though a god had just appeared,
A golden face those darker ones surround.

Their chorus of surprise, almost a chant,
Their laughter and the music of the fifes—
They reach us not as sound, but shapes of sound.
Their arms, thrown open, multiply and break,
Their widened gestures dilate and dissolve,
And color molts from shade to shade
Beyond all color, without end,
Spinning islands in the air
And shattered organ-pipes of cloud. Is this
The resurrection of the dead? Then it must be
The final cresting of the waves, before they tumble down.
The sky is almost empty now.
A ruddy mass slouches north
Toward a curtain of black birds, twittering: night.

Here and there
A puddle struck by an ember
Of beauty burnt to ash.

DE VENT ET DE FUMÉE

I

L'Idée, a-t-on pensé, est la mesure de tout,
D'où suit que « la sua bella Helena rapita », dit Bellori
D'une célèbre peinture de Guido Reni,
Peut être comparée à l'autre Hélène,
Celle qu'imagina, aima peut-être, Zeuxis.
Mais que sont des images auprès de la jeune femme
Que Pâris a tant désirée ? La seule vigne,
N'est-ce pas le frémissement des mains réelles
Sous la fièvre des lèvres ? Et que l'enfant
Demande avidement à la grappe, et boive
À même la lumière, en hâte, avant
Que le temps ne déferle sur ce qui est ?

Mais non,
A pensé un commentateur de l'*Iliade,* anxieux
D'expliquer, d'excuser dix ans de guerre,
Et le vrai, c'est qu'Hélène ne fut pas
Assaillie, ne fut pas transportée de barque en vaisseau,
Ne fut pas retenue, criante, enchaînée
Sur des lits en désordre. Le ravisseur
N'emportait qu'une image : une statue
Que l'art d'un magicien avait faite des brises
Des soirées de l'été quand tout est calme,
Pour qu'elle eût la tiédeur du corps en vie
Et même sa respiration, et le regard

FROM WIND AND SMOKE

I

The Idea, some have thought, is the measure of all things.
If that were true, then Guido Reni's famous painting—
"La sua bella Elena rapita," Bellori called it—
Might compare to the other Helen: the Helen
Zeuxis depicted; the Helen he may have loved.
But what are such images, beside the real
Woman desired by Paris? Isn't the actual vine
This trembling of hands under fever's lips?
Why else would a child demand these grapes
So greedily? Why else would he make haste
To gulp the cluster down, to drink the light
Before the flood of time unfurls?

No, not at all, a commentator wrote,
Anxious to explain away
Ten years of war in the *Iliad.*
The truth is, Helen was never kidnapped;
She wasn't dragged, screaming, from boat to ship,
And chained to roughed-up beds.
An image was all the ravisher carried off,
A statue wrought by some magician's art
From the calm breezes of a summer eve:
So she would radiate their warmth,
And breathe with them like flesh—

Qui se prête au désir. La feinte Hélène
Erre rêveusement sous les voûtes basses
Du navire qui fuit, il semble qu'elle écoute
Le bruit de l'autre mer dans ses veines bleues
Et qu'elle soit heureuse. D'autres scoliastes
Ont même cru à une œuvre de pierre.
Dans la cabine
Jour après jour secouée par le gros temps
Hélène est figurée, à demi levée
De ses draps, de ses rêves,
Elle sourit, ou presque. Son bras est reployé
Avec beaucoup de grâce sur son sein,
Les rayons du soleil, levant, couchant,
S'attardent puis s'effacent sur son flanc nu.
Et plus tard, sur la terrasse de Troie,
Elle a toujours ce sourire.
Qui pourtant, sauf Pâris peut-être, l'a jamais vue ?
Les porteurs n'auront su que la grande pierre rougeâtre,
Rugueuse, fissurée
Qu'il leur fallut monter, suant, jurant,
Jusque sur les remparts, devant la nuit.

Cette roche,
Ce sable de l'origine, qui se délite,
Est-ce Hélène ? Ces nuages, ces lueurs rouges
On ne sait si dans l'âme ou dans le ciel ?

So her eyes would reflect desire.
Helen's effigy
Wanders dreaming through the low arches
Of the fleeing ship. She seems to hear
The purling of another sea
In her blue veins; she seems content.
Other scholiasts have even thought
She was a sculpture made of stone.
In the cabin, jostled by squalls
Day after day, Helen's figure
Lies half risen from her sheets,
Or from her dreams—and smiling,
Almost. She folds an arm
Gracefully against her breast.
The rising sun, the setting sun
Meander on her nakedness,
Then fade away. Later, on the high
Terrace of Troy, she keeps that smile.
But who—besides Paris, perhaps—
Has ever seen her? All the bearers knew
Was a huge reddish stone, cracked and rugged.
Cursing, drenched in sweat, they had to haul it
To the ramparts, in front of night.

A crumbling rock, the sand of origin:
Is this Helen, then? These clouds, these ruddy gleams:
Are they in the soul, or the sky?

La vérité peut-être, mais gardée tue,
Même Stésichorus ne l'avoue pas,
Voici : la semblance d'Hélène ne fut qu'un feu
Bâti contre le vent sur une plage.
C'est une masse de branches grises, de fumées
(Car le feu prenait mal) que Pâris a chargée
Au petit jour humide sur la barque.
C'est ce brasier, ravagé par les vagues,
Cerné par la clameur des oiseaux de mer,
Qu'il restitua au monde, sur les brisants
Du rivage natal, que ravagent et trouent
D'autres vagues encore. Le lit de pierre
Avait été dressé là-haut, de par le ciel,
Et quand Troie tomberait resterait le feu
Pour crier la beauté, la protestation de l'esprit
Contre la mort.

Nuées,
L'une qui prend à l'autre, qui défend
Mal, qui répand
Entre ces corps épris
La coupe étincelante de la foudre.

Et le ciel
S'est attardé, un peu,
Sur la couche terrestre. On dirait, apaisés,
L'homme, la femme : une montagne, une eau.

Even Stesichorus wouldn't admit
The truth; but maybe it was this:
Helen's semblance was just a fire,
Built against the wind on a beach—
A skein of gray branches and smoke
From sputtering flames. At the dew-point
Of dawn, Paris heaped the sodden bonfire
On a boat, ravaged by waves and ringed
By screeching seabirds.
He kindled it again on his native shores,
Where breakers slashed and gouged
The shoals anew. Above, against the sky,
He'd raised the bed of stone.
The day Troy fell, a fire would remain
To shout of beauty—the only protest
Of the spirit against death.

Clouds . . .
One catches at another, that can't resist.
And between these bodies in love,
From its glittering cup,
A thunderbolt spills out.

The sky
Lingers for a while
On the bed of earth. The water, the mountain:
They seem like a woman, a man.

Entre eux
La coupe déjà vide, encore pleine.

II

Mais qui a dit
Que celle que Pâris a étreint, le feu,
Les branches rouges dans le feu, l'âcre fumée
Dans les orbites vides, ne fut pas même
Ce rêve, qui se fait œuvre pour calmer
Le désir de l'artiste, mais simplement
Un rêve de ce rêve ? Le sourire d'Hélène :
Rien que ce glissement du drap de la nuit, qui montre,
Mais pour rien qu'un éclair,
La lumière endormie en bas du ciel.

Chaque fois qu'un poème,
Une statue, même une image peinte,
Se préfèrent figure, se dégagent
Des à-coups d'étincellement de la nuée,
Hélène se dissipe, qui ne fut
Que l'intuition qui fit se pencher Homère
Sur des sons de plus bas que ses cordes dans
La maladroite lyre des mots terrestres.

Mais à l'aube du sens
Quand la pierre est encore obscure, la couleur
Boue, dans l'impatience du pinceau,
Pâris emporte Hélène,

Between them,
The cup is already empty, and still full.

II

But this woman Paris embraced—this fire
And the branches red within the fire,
The hollow sockets bitter with smoke—
Who can say? Was she the dream
Behind the work that slakes the artist's thirst—
Or merely a dream of that dream?
Helen's smile: only a fold in the cloth of night,
Slipping to reveal how light still sleeps
Beneath the sky,
For a lightning flash.

Helen melts away
Every time a poem,
A statue, even a painted image
Tries to become a figure, detached
From the fits and starts of the gleaming cloud.
She was merely an intuition Homer sought,
Plumbing the notes below his deepest strings
On the awkward lyre of earthly words.

But at the dawn of meaning—
When the stone is still obscure, when color
Is still mud in the headlong brush—
Paris does carry Helen off;

Elle se débat, elle crie,
Elle accepte ; et les vagues sont calmes, contre l'étrave,
Et l'aube est rayonnante sur la mer.

Bois, dit Pâris
Qui s'éveille, et étend le bras dans l'ombre étroite
De la chambre remuée par le peu de houle,
Bois,
Puis approche la coupe de mes lèvres
Pour que je puisse boire.

Je me penche, répond
Celle qui est, peut-être, ou dont il rêve.
Je me penche, je bois,
Je n'ai pas plus de nom que la nuée,
Je me déchire comme elle, lumière pure.

Et t'ayant donné joie je n'ai plus de soif,
Lumière bue.

C'est un enfant
Nu sur la grande plage quand Troie brûlait
Qui le dernier vit Hélène
Dans les buissons de flammes du haut des murs.
Il errait, il chantait,
Il avait pris dans ses mains un peu d'eau,
Le feu venait y boire, mais l'eau s'échappe

And though she struggles and cries out,
She accepts. The hull moves calmly
Through the waves, like daybreak
Across the sea.

Drink, says Paris,
When he wakes, stretching out his arm,
As the cabin's narrow darkness
Rocks in a gentle swell.
Drink—
Then raise the cup to my lips
So I can drink as well.

I will, she answers; I will drink.
(Does she exist, or only as a dream?)
I have no name, no more than a cloud.
A cloud, I will dissolve in purest light.

And once I have given you joy, the light
Consumed, I will never thirst again.

From the wide beach, the day Troy burned,
A naked child
Was the last to see her: Helen,
A tree of flames on the upper wall.
He dawdled, he sang.
He cupped a little water in his hands,
Where the fire could come to drink.

De la coupe imparfaite, ainsi le temps
Ruine le rêve et pourtant le rédime.

III

Ces pages sont traduites. D'une langue
Qui hante la mémoire que je suis.
Les phrases de cette langue sont incertaines
Comme les tout premiers de nos souvenirs.
J'ai restitué le texte mot après mot,
Mais le mien n'en sera qu'une ombre, c'est à croire
Que l'origine est une Troie qui brûle,
La beauté un regret, l'œuvre ne prendre
À pleines mains qu'une eau qui se refuse.

But water seeps from the imperfect cup:
The dream is ruined by time; by time redeemed.

III

These pages are translations. From a tongue
That haunts the memory I have become.
Its phrases falter, like what we recollect
From early childhood, long ago.
I built the text again, word for word:
But mine is only shadow. As though we know
All origin is a Troy that burns,
All beauty but regret, and all our work
Runs like water through our hands.

UNE PIERRE

J'ai toujours faim de ce lieu
Qui nous était un miroir,
Des fruits voûtés dans son eau,
De sa lumière qui sauve,

Et je graverai dans la pierre
En souvenir qu'il brilla
Un cercle, ce feu désert.
Au-dessus le ciel est rapide

Comme au vœu la pierre est fermée.
Que cherchions-nous ? Rien peut-être,
Une passion n'est qu'un rêve,
Ses mains ne demandent pas.

Et de qui aima une image,
Le regard a beau désirer,
La voix demeure brisée,
La parole est pleine de cendres.

A STONE

I still hunger for that place
That was our mirror, hunger
For the fruit curved in its waters,
Hunger for its saving light.

And in memory of how it shone,
I will now engrave a circle
On the rock, an empty fire.
The sky moves swiftly overhead,

As the stone closes to our vow.
What were we seeking? Nothing,
Perhaps. A passion is only a dream;
Its hands will never ask.

And whoever has loved an image:
Though his eyes may still desire,
His voice is broken;
His words are full of ash.

LE CANOT DE SAMUEL BECKETT

L'île est peu loin du rivage, c'est une étendue sans relief dont on devine à peine la ligne basse, avec quelques arbres, dans la brume qui pèse sur la mer. Quelqu'un dont nous ne savons rien, sinon la bienveillance et qu'il a voulu que nous venions là, nous a pris dans sa barque, nous sommes partis mais il pleut et traverser le bras d'eau ressemble, sous le voile des ombres souvent très noires, à une trouée dans les apparences, au rêve d'un autre monde, peut-être à déjà un peu de celui-ci, faible rayon dans les taches sombres. Une rive pourtant, au bout de quelques minutes. Trois ou quatre marches de pierre pour le débarquement, ruisselantes, un bout de quai, deux petites maisons et dans l'une une lumière : le pub fermé et le logis de qui tient le pub et l'ouvre parfois, le dimanche, quand des paysans de l'autre île, celle dont nous venons, veulent se porter vers plus d'ouest encore. Mais nous ne nous approchons pas des maisons, nous passons à droite par les terres. Ce sont des chemins détrempés ou même pas de chemin, une lande alors, coupée de flaques si ce n'est barrée par du fil de fer, qu'il faut enjamber, bien péniblement. Où allons-nous, je ne sais, comprenant mal le rude et superbe accent de cette voix en son autre langue. Peut-être est-ce vers quelque croix de pierre des temps celtiques, dressée devant le large, peut-être seulement vers l'autre côté de l'île que nous venons en effet d'atteindre. Voici le rebord, de grosses vagues sont devant nous, très vertes, et la pluie a cessé, ou presque.

Nous sommes restés un moment, au bout de l'île. Nous admirons la mer, nous regardons aussi le chemin qui fut suivi, ou parfois laissé, à cause des trous ou sans raison : ce ne fut rien qu'une sorte de piste qui

BECKETT'S DINGHY

The island isn't far from the coast: it's a flat line hard to make out, topped by several trees, in the fog that hunkers down on the sea. All we know about the man who's taking us there in his boat is that he's kindly offered to show us around. It's raining when we push off, and we cross the narrow sound under a veil of inky shadows. We seem to be punching a hole in appearances, dreaming another world; and maybe we've almost reached it: a dim glimmer in the splotches of darkness. But after a few minutes, here's the shore. A tiny landing, where you disembark on three or four steps, hewn from glistening stone. Two little buildings, a light in one: the shut-up pub and the pub-keeper's house. He opens it on Sundays now and then, for the farmers from the other island, when they want to travel even farther west. But we don't approach the buildings; we go inland, to the right. The path is sodden—when there's a path at all—and we slog through a puddle-infested moor. We have to pick our way over barbed-wire fences—no easy feat. I scarcely understand our guide's rough, splendid accent, in a language foreign to me. Who knows where we're really headed: maybe to a stone cross from Celtic times, facing the surf; maybe just to the far side of the island. And in fact, now we've reached it. Here's the outer edge, with stout green waves in front of us; the rain has almost stopped.

We stay there for a while, at the tip of the island, admiring the ocean. We also look back at the path we've followed, or sidestepped—because of the holes, or for no reason at all. It's just a vague track that

zigzague dans l'herbe pauvre, bordée par endroits de murets de pierre. Puis, nous nous engageons sur un autre, un plus large sentier, qui suit la côte. Notre guide, notre ami, parle, je le comprends mieux maintenant, parce que la mer fait moins de bruit, parce que la marche s'est faite plus facile, peut-être aussi parce qu'il a d'autres pensées en esprit, et voici en tout cas qu'une maison, il y en a donc une troisième dans l'île, se découvre derrière un arbre : et à deux pas d'elle, c'est l'océan, mais elle a son petit enclos, il y a eu là autrefois des pommes de terre, des salades, du persil, sans doute aussi quelques fleurs à l'abri d'un peu de rocher. « Ah, nous dit le marin — c'est un marin, chaque année, vient-il d'expliquer, il mène un cargo autour du monde —, cette vieille qui vivait là ! Quand j'étais enfant elle m'avait fait l'école. Et plus tard, pendant si longtemps plus tard, quand je passais par ici, de nuit, je frappais toujours à sa porte. Il pouvait être minuit, deux heures, trois, presque l'aube, je la savais éveillée, habillée, debout ou dans son fauteuil près du feu, et voilà qu'elle m'ouvrait, me riait, me servait du thé, me racontait des histoires. Elle avait sans fin des histoires. »

« Elle n'est plus », ajoute celui qui se souvient ainsi puis se tait, comme s'il écoutait une voix. Nous arrivons au hameau, les deux maisons, et il veut absolument nous faire visiter le pub, il va frapper à l'autre porte, une jeune femme paraît, un enfant, il revient avec la clef, il tâtonne dans la serrure. Nous entrons dans la salle, où il fait très sombre, où il allume une lampe. Les tables contre le mur, le comptoir usuel, avec les bouteilles, sans doute vides. Le grand plancher nu, très usé, comme si on y avait dansé des milliers de fois dans un passé qui ne touche plus à notre présent, eau qui s'est retirée du rivage. Et des

weaves through the scrubby grass, bordered here and there by low walls of stone. Then we set out on a wider trail that hugs the coast. Our guide, our friend, goes on talking. Since the surf's not as loud and the walking is easier, I understand him better now—perhaps because he's also turned to other thoughts. At any rate, tucked behind a tree, we come upon another house: so there's a third one on the island. It's only a couple of steps from the sea, but it has a small enclosure. Lettuce, parsley, and potatoes used to grow there; some flowers as well, sheltered by a wedge of rock. "Oh, the old lady who lived here!" the mariner says. He's a seaman, he just explained to us, and every year he carries a cargo around the world. "When I was a child, she taught me in school; and later, for a long, long time, when I'd pass this way at night, I always knocked on her door. No matter if it was midnight, one or two in the morning, or almost dawn, I knew she'd be awake and dressed. She'd either be pottering around or sitting in her armchair next to the fire. And she'd open the door, laugh, and serve me some tea while she told me her stories. She had tons of them."

He reminisces, but then falls silent, as though he's listening to a voice. "She's no longer with us," he adds. We've circled back to the hamlet, the first pair of buildings. He insists we visit the pub. He knocks on the other door: a young woman with a child appears. He returns with the key, and jiggles it in the lock. We enter the pitch-black room, and he lights a lamp. Tables against the wall, the usual bar—though the bottles are empty, no doubt. The broad, bare floor seems worn, as though people had danced there thousands of times: in a past removed from our present, like water that's retreated far from shore.

photographies sur les murs, qui sont la raison de notre visite, car c'est la communauté d'autrefois qu'elles nous diront, la société des deux îles qui peu à peu s'est dispersée, s'est éteinte. Des hommes et des femmes de l'autre brume, celle du papier qui a jauni comme une métaphore de la mémoire qui se dissipe. Quelques regards qui se portent sur nous, qui nous font reproche, distraitement, comme s'ils étaient occupés plus loin par une vision, peut-être un savoir, que nous ne pouvons plus faire nôtres. L'Irlande des années 40 ou 50, aussi mystérieuse qu'un bateau cherchant le rivage.

« Et celui-la », s'exclame le capitaine au long cours, en nous montrant la photographie d'un vieil homme assis devant l'eau, sa pipe à la main, très droit, très maigre, tout immobile. « Ah, ce qu'il buvait ! Pour pêcher le homard il partait pour des jours, seul dans sa petite barque, mais déjà au départ il était ivre, parmi les flacons de whisky qu'il emportait avec lui parmi les paniers, les filets ! Comment s'y prenait-il pour affronter le gros temps, pour revenir, il revenait, cependant, il était dans la main de Dieu. »

Je regarde ce beau visage, qui ressemble à celui de Samuel Beckett, j'oublie l'alcool, qui n'est qu'une des techniques de l'universelle écriture — cette main qui cherche celle de Dieu —, je pense a l'écrivain qui vient de se glisser, lui aussi, parmi les ombres, et s'éloigne et se perd dans cette foule noircie de pluie, ou de brume, mais que désassombrit, tout de même, ici et là, et là-bas encore, un peu de lumière de soleil jaune. Beckett, me dis-je, a écrit comme ce vieil homme partait, seul sur la mer. Il est resté comme lui de longues journées et des nuits sous ces nuages d'ici qui s'amoncellent, se font châteaux dans le ciel, falaises, dragons crachant du feu à des rebords, dans des

We're here to see the photographs on the wall; they're supposed to tell us about the former inhabitants of these two islands, before their community scattered and died out. Men and women dwell in another bank of fog: this paper that yellows and fades, like a metaphor of memory. Some of their faces stare back at us, distractedly reproachful, as though absorbed by a faraway vision—a knowledge, perhaps—that we can no longer share. Ireland from the forties and fifties, mysterious as a ship skirting the coast.

"And that one there, what a drinker he was!" the long-distance captain exclaims. The picture shows an old man seated in front of the ocean, pipe in hand: skinny, upright, stock-still. "He'd cast off and catch lobsters for days on end, alone in his little dinghy. But he'd already be drunk before he left, and he'd stow flasks of whiskey with his nets and baskets. How on earth did he buck the worst of the weather and come back? Well, he always came back, so he must've been in God's own hand."

I look at the beautiful face, which resembles Samuel Beckett's. And I forget about the alcohol: merely a device of universal writing, this hand that seeks the hand of God. I think how the writer, too, has just vanished in the distance. He's slipped away into the throng of shadows, blackened by rain or fog; though here and there—and over there again—we glimpse a streak of yellow sun. Beckett, I tell myself, wrote the way that old man sailed, alone on the sea. Like him, he spent long days and nights beneath the clouds I've watched here, piling up as castles in the sky, as cliffs, with dragons spitting fire from their ridges and crevasses. Suddenly, they shear apart before a sweeping beam, a

failles, et soudain se défont, rayon soudain, « spell of light » vers trois heures de l'après-midi, — et c'est alors jusqu'au soir rapide le temps qui cesse, c'est comme de l'or dans les faibles creux de la houle. Beckett est là-bas maintenant, dans ce canot parfois peut-être encore presque visible là où la crête de l'océan s'ébouriffe dans le soleil qui se couche. Et ce que disent ses livres, ne l'écoutons qu'au travers du bruit constant de la vague, ou intermittent de la pluie.

"spell of light," around three in the afternoon. From then until the evening swiftly falls, time slows to a halt, and gold seems to lie in the ocean's gentle hollows. Beckett is far from us now, though his boat is still dimly visible: maybe over there, where sunset ruffles a crest of sea. We should listen to his books only through the constant roll of waves, the intermittent drumming of the rain.

FROM LES PLANCHES COURBES

THE CURVED PLANKS

UNE PIERRE

Matins que nous avions,
Je retirais les cendres, j'allais emplir
Le broc, je le posais sur le dallage,
Avec lui ruisselait dans toute la salle
L'odeur impénétrable de la menthe.

Ô souvenir,
Tes arbres sont en fleurs devant le ciel,
On peut croire qu'il neige,
Mais la foudre s'éloigne sur le chemin,
Le vent du soir répand son trop de graines.

A STONE

Those mornings of ours,
I would sweep up the ashes; I would fill
The jug and set it on the flagstones,
So the whole room was awash
With the fathomless smell of mint.

O memory,
Your trees blossom against the sky:
We could almost believe that it's snowing.
But thunder retreats down the path.
The evening wind sheds its excess seeds.

UNE PIERRE

Tout était pauvre, nu, transfigurable,
Nos meubles étaient simples comme des pierres,
Nous aimions que la fente dans le mur
Fût cet épi dont essaimaient des mondes.

Nuées, ce soir,
Les mêmes que toujours, comme la soif,
La même étoffe rouge, dégrafée.
Imagine, passant,
Nos recommencements, nos hâtes, nos confiances.

A STONE

Spare, bare, transfigurable: the things
In our rooms were simple as stones.
We loved the crevice in the wall, a bursting
Ear of grain that spilled out worlds.

Clouds, this evening,
The same as always, like thirst,
The same red dress, unfastened.
Imagine, passer-by,
Our new beginnings, our eagerness, our trust.

UNE PIERRE

Une hâte mystérieuse nous appelait.
Nous sommes entrés, nous avons ouvert
Les volets, nous avons reconnu la table, l'âtre,
Le lit ; l'étoile grandissait à la croisée,
Nous entendions la voix qui veut que l'on aime
Au plus haut de l'été
Comme jouent les dauphins dans leur eau sans rive.

Dormons, ne nous sachant. Sein contre sein,
Souffles mêlés, main dans la main sans rêves.

A STONE

A mysterious haste urged us on.
We went in, we opened
The shutters, we recognized the table, the hearth,
The bed; the star was growing larger in the window,
We heard the voice that wants us to love
At summer's crest
Like dolphins playing in their sea without a shore.

Unknowing, let us sleep. Chest against chest,
Our breathing mingled, hand in hand without dreams.

UNE PIERRE

Nous nous étions fait don de l'innocence,
Elle a brûlé longtemps de rien que nos deux corps,
Et nos pas allaient nus dans l'herbe sans mémoire,
Nous étions l'illusion qu'on nomme souvenir.

Le feu naissant de soi, pourquoi vouloir
En rassembler les cendres désunies.
Au jour dit nous avons rendu ce que nous fûmes
À la flamme plus vaste du ciel du soir.

A STONE

We granted each other the gift of innocence:
For years, only our two bodies fed its flames.
Our steps wandered bare through trackless grass.
We were the illusion known as memory.

Since fire is born of fire, why should we want
To gather up its scattered ash.
On the appointed day we surrendered what we were
To a vaster blaze, the evening sky.

UNE PIERRE

Nos ombres devant nous, sur le chemin,
Avaient couleur, par la grâce de l'herbe,
Elles eurent rebond, contre des pierres.

Et des ombres d'oiseaux les effleuraient
En criant, ou bien s'attardaient, là où nos fronts
Se penchaient l'un vers l'autre, se touchant presque
Du fait de mots que nous voulions nous dire.

A STONE

The grass granted color to our shadows,
Before us on the path; and once
They rebounded on some stones.

Bird-shadows, too, brushed by them
With a cry, or lingered where our foreheads
Leaned together so we almost touched
Because of words we wanted to share.

UNE PIERRE

Plus de chemins pour nous, rien que l'herbe haute,
Plus de passage à gué, rien que la boue,
Plus de lit préparé, rien que l'étreinte
À travers nous des ombres et des pierres.

Mais claire cette nuit
Comme nous désirions que fût notre mort.
Elle blanchit les arbres, ils s'élargissent.
Leur feuillage : du sable, puis de l'écume.
Même au-delà du temps le jour se lève.

A STONE

No more paths for us, nothing but unscythed grass.
No more ford to cross, nothing but mud.
No more bed laid out, nothing but stones
And shadows embracing through us.

Still this night is bright,
As we desired our death might be.
It whitens the trees, they expand.
Their foliage: sand, then foam.
Day is breaking, even beyond time.

UNE PIERRE

Ils ont vécu au temps ou les mots furent pauvres,
Le sens ne vibrait plus dans les rythmes défaits,
La fumée foisonnait, enveloppant la flamme,
Ils craignaient que la joie ne les surprendrait plus.

Ils ont dormi. Ce fut par détresse du monde.
Passaient dans leur sommeil des souvenirs
Comme des barques dans la brume, qui accroissent
Leurs feux, avant de prendre le haut du fleuve.

Ils se sont éveillés. Mais l'herbe est déjà noire.
Les ombres soient leur pain et le vent leur eau.
Le silence, l'inconnaissance leur anneau,
Une brassée de nuit tout leur feu sur terre.

A STONE

They lived in the time when words were poor.
In rhythms undone, meaning pulsed no longer.
Smoke billowed up and shrouded the flame.
They feared that joy would not surprise them again.

They slept and slept, distressed by the world.
Memories passed through their sleep
Like boats in the fog, stoking their fires
Before they head upstream.

They woke. But the grass had already turned black.
Let wind be their water, and shadow their bread,
Unknowing and silence their ring.
An armful of night all their fire on earth.

UNE PIERRE

Il se souvient
De quand deux mains terrestres attiraient
Sa tête, la pressaient
Sur des genoux de chaleur éternelle.

Étale le désir ces jours, parmi ses rêves,
Silencieux le peu de houle de sa vie,
Les doigts illuminés gardaient clos ses yeux.

Mais le soleil du soir, la barque des morts,
Touchait la vitre, et demandait rivage.

A STONE

He remembers
When two earthly hands
Held his head
On knees of eternal warmth.

Those days of becalmed desire, among his dreams,
The mild sea-swell of his life all silent,
Glowing fingers kept his eyes shut.

But the evening sun, the skiff of the dead,
Was touching the window, asking for berth.

UNE PIERRE

Les livres, ce qu'il déchira,
La page dévastée, mais la lumière
Sur la page, l'accroissement de la lumière,
Il comprit qu'il redevenait la page blanche.

Il sortit. La figure du monde, déchirée,
Lui parut d'une beauté autre, plus humaine.
La main du ciel cherchait sa main dans le jeu des ombres,
La pierre, où vous voyez que son nom s'efface,
S'entrouvrait, se faisait une parole.

A STONE

The books: he tore them all apart.
The devastated page. Yet the light
On the page, the increase of light. He knew
He was becoming the blank page again.

He went out. Torn, the visage of the world
Took on another beauty, seemed more human now.
In shadow play, the sky's hand reached for his.
The stone where you see his weathered name
Was opening, forming a word.

« PASSANT, CE SONT DES MOTS ... »

Passant, ce sont des mots. Mais plutôt que lire
Je veux que tu écoutes : cette frêle
Voix comme en ont les lettres que l'herbe mange.

Prête l'oreille, entends d'abord l'heureuse abeille
Butiner dans nos noms presque effacés.
Elle erre de l'un à l'autre des deux feuillages,
Portant le bruit des ramures réelles
À celles qui ajourent l'or invisible.

Puis sache un bruit plus faible encore, et que ce soit
Le murmure sans fin de toutes nos ombres.
Il monte, celui-ci, de sous les pierres
Pour ne faire qu'une chaleur avec l'aveugle
Lumière que tu es encore, ayant regard.

Simple te soit l'écoute ! Le silence
Est un seuil où, par voie de ce rameau
Qui casse imperceptiblement sous ta main qui cherche
À dégager un nom sur une pierre,

Nos noms absents désenchevêtrent tes alarmes,
Et pour toi qui t'éloignes, pensivement,
Ici devient là-bas sans cesser d'être.

"PASSER-BY, THESE ARE WORDS . . ."

Passer-by, these are words. But instead of reading
I want you to listen: to this frail
Voice like that of letters eaten by grass.

Lend an ear, hear first of all the happy bee
Foraging in our almost rubbed-out names.
It flits between two sprays of leaves,
Carrying the sound of branches that are real
To those that filigree the unseen gold.

Then know an even fainter sound, and let it be
The endless murmuring of all our shades.
Their whisper rises from beneath the stones
To fuse into a single heat with that blind
Light you are as yet, who can still gaze.

Listen simply, if you will. Silence is a threshold
Where, unfelt, a twig is breaking in your hand
As you try to disengage
A name upon a stone:

And so our absent names untangle your alarms.
And for you who now move on, pensively,
Here becomes there without ceasing to be.

LA PLUIE SUR LE RAVIN

I

Il pleut, sur le ravin, sur le monde. Les huppes
Se sont posées sur notre grange, cimes
De colonnes errantes de fumée.
Aube, consens à nous aujourd'hui encore.

De la première guêpe
J'ai entendu l'éveil, déjà, dans la tiédeur
De la brume qui ferme le chemin
Où quelques flaques brillent. Dans sa paix
Elle cherche, invisible. Je pourrais croire
Que je suis là, que je l'écoute. Mais son bruit
Ne s'accroît qu'en image. Mais sous mes pas
Le chemin n'est plus le chemin, rien que mon rêve
De la guêpe, des huppes, de la brume.

J'aimais sortir à l'aube. Le temps dormait
Dans les braises, le front contre la cendre.
Dans la chambre d'en haut respiraient en paix
Nos corps que découvrait la décrue des ombres.

II

Pluie des matins d'été, inoubliable
Clapotement comme d'un premier froid

RAIN FALLS ON THE RAVINE

I

Rain falls on the ravine, on the world.
Hoopoes alighting on our barn
Crown wandering columns of smoke.
Dawn, consent to us once more today.

I hear the first wasp
Already rousing in the warmth
Of the fog that seals this path
Where a few puddles shine. The wasp searches
In peace, invisible. I could believe
That I am here, that I listen; but its hum
Deepens only in my mind. The path
Beneath my feet is no longer the path,
Only my dream
Of the wasp, the hoopoes, the fog.

I liked setting out at dawn. Time lay asleep
In the embers, forehead pressed against the ashes.
In the room upstairs the shadows' ebb
Uncovered our bodies, breathing in peace.

II

Rain of summer mornings, plashing
Unforgettably, like a first chill

Sur la vitre du rêve ; et le dormeur
Se déprenait de soi et demandait
À mains nues dans ce bruit de la pluie sur le monde
L'autre corps, qui dormait encore, et sa chaleur.

(Bruit de l'eau sur le toit de tuiles, par rafales,
Avancée de la chambre par à-coups
Dans la houle, qui s'enfle, de la lumière.
L'orage
A envahi le ciel, l'éclair
S'est fait d'un grand cri bref,
Et les richesses de la foudre se répandent.)

III

Je me lève, je vois
Que notre barque a tourné, cette nuit.
Le feu est presque éteint.
Le froid pousse le ciel d'un coup de rame.

Et la surface de l'eau n'est que lumière,
Mais au-dessous ? Troncs d'arbres sans couleur, rameaux
Enchevêtrés comme le rêve, pierres
Dont le courant rapide a clos les yeux
Et qui sourient dans l'étreinte du sable.

On the windowpane of dream.
The sleeper, parting from himself
In this rain that pelted the world,
Asked with naked hands for the other body,
Still asleep, and for its heat.

(Squalls slap the roof tiles,
The room thrusts ahead by fits and starts
In the surging swell of light.
The storm
Has invaded the sky, lightning
Cracks with a loud shout
And the riches of the thunderbolt pour out.)

III

I get up and see that our boat
Has veered in the night.
The fire has died down.
The chill pushes the sky with a flick of its oar.

The water's surface is light alone.
But underneath? Faded tree-trunks,
Boughs entangled like a dream, stones
With eyes the rapid stream has closed
And that smile in the sand's embrace.

LA MAISON NATALE

I

Je m'éveillai, c'était la maison natale,
L'écume s'abattait sur le rocher,
Pas un oiseau, le vent seul à ouvrir et fermer la vague,
L'odeur de l'horizon de toutes parts,
Cendre, comme si les collines cachaient un feu
Qui ailleurs consumait un univers.
Je passai dans la véranda, la table était mise,
L'eau frappait les pieds de la table, le buffet.
Il fallait qu'elle entrât pourtant, la sans-visage
Que je savais qui secouait la porte
Du couloir, du côté de l'escalier sombre, mais en vain,
Si haute était déjà l'eau dans la salle.
Je tournais la poignée, qui résistait,
J'entendais presque les rumeurs de l'autre rive,
Ces rires des enfants dans l'herbe haute.
Ces jeux des autres, à jamais les autres, dans leur joie.

II

Je m'éveillai, c'était la maison natale.
Il pleuvait doucement dans toutes les salles,
J'allais d'une à une autre, regardant
L'eau qui étincelait sur les miroirs
Amoncelés partout, certains brisés ou même
Poussés entre des meubles et les murs.
C'était de ces reflets que, parfois, un visage

THE HOUSE WHERE I WAS BORN

I

I woke: the house where I was born.
Spume battered the rock. Not a bird;
Only wind, closing and opening the wave.
The horizon all around smelled of ash,
As though somewhere beyond the hills
A fire were devouring a universe. I went
Into the side room: the table had been set.
Water struck the sideboard, the table legs.
Yet she had to come in, the faceless one;
I knew she was rattling the hallway door,
There near the darkened stairs. But in vain:
Water was already flooding the room.
I turned the knob; the door wouldn't give.
I almost heard them on that far-off shore—
Children laughing in high grass. Others
Laughing, always others, in their joy.

II

I woke: the house where I was born.
Rain was falling softly in all the rooms.
I went from room to room, looking
At the water as it sparkled on the mirrors
Piled up everywhere—some shattered, others
Even tucked between the furniture and walls.
At times in those reflections I could see

Se dégageait, riant, d'une douceur
De plus et autrement que ce qu'est le monde.
Et je touchais, hésitant, dans l'image,
Les mèches désordonnées de la déesse,
Je découvrais sous le voile de l'eau
Son front triste et distrait de petite fille.
Étonnement entre être et ne pas être,
Main qui hésite à toucher la buée,
Puis j'écoutais le rire s'éloigner
Dans les couloirs de la maison déserte.
Ici rien qu'à jamais le bien du rêve,
La main tendue qui ne traverse pas
L'eau rapide, où s'efface le souvenir.

III

Je m'éveillai, c'était la maison natale,
Il faisait nuit, des arbres se pressaient
De toutes parts autour de notre porte,
J'étais seul sur le seuil dans le vent froid,
Mais non, nullement seul, car deux grands êtres
Se parlaient au-dessus de moi, à travers moi.
L'un, derrière, une vieille femme, courbe, mauvaise,
L'autre debout dehors comme une lampe,
Belle, tenant la coupe qu'on lui offrait,
Buvant avidement de toute sa soif.
Ai-je voulu me moquer, certes non,
Plutôt ai-je poussé un cri d'amour
Mais avec la bizarrerie du désespoir,

A face appear, laughing with a sweetness
Other than the world's, beyond its ken.
And hesitant, in the image I touched
The disheveled tresses of the goddess;
Through the veil of water I beheld
Her sad, distracted brow of a little girl.
Perplexity between what is and what
Is not, hand that hesitates on misted glass . . .
Then I listened as the laughter trailed away
Down the corridors of the deserted house.
Here the only thing we ever own is dream:
Though we reach out, our hand can never cross
The rapid stream where memories recede.

III

I woke: the house where I was born.
In the night, on every side, trees
Crowded round our door. I stood there
On the threshold, alone in the freezing wind.
But no, not alone at all. Two large figures
Were speaking above me, speaking through me:
One was an old woman, evil and stooped;
The other stood outside, radiant as a lamp,
Raising the cup that had been offered her.
Eagerly she drank, with all her thirst.
Did I mean to mock her? Surely not.
The strangled sound I made was a cry of love,
But it rang with the strangeness of despair.

Et le poison fut partout dans mes membres,
Cérès moquée brisa qui l'avait aimée.
Ainsi parle aujourd'hui la vie murée dans la vie.

IV

Une autre fois.
Il faisait nuit encore. De l'eau glissait
Silencieusement sur le sol noir,
Et je savais que je n'aurais pour tâche
Que de me souvenir, et je riais,
Je me penchais, je prenais dans la boue
Une brassée de branches et de feuilles,
J'en soulevais la masse, qui ruisselait
Dans mes bras resserrés contre mon cœur.
Que faire de ce bois où de tant d'absence
Montait pourtant le bruit de la couleur,
Peu importe, j'allais en hâte, à la recherche
D'au moins quelque hangar, sous cette charge
De branches qui avaient de toute part
Des angles, des élancements, des pointes, des cris.

Et des voix, qui jetaient des ombres sur la route,
Ou m'appelaient, et je me retournais,
Le cœur précipité, sur la route vide.

And then the poison seized me, head to toe.
Mocked, Ceres doomed the one who loved her:
So says today the life that's walled inside of life.

IV

Another time.
Night again. In silence
Water slid on the darkened ground.
I knew the only task I would have
Was to remember. And laughing,
Bending over in the mud, I gathered up
An armful of branches and leaves.
I held them to my chest; they dripped
As I clutched them against my heart.
What should I do with this wood,
Where so much absence
Still rang with color's sound?
It didn't matter. I hurried on,
Looking for a shed at least, reeling
Under branches that bristled with snags,
Throbbing hopes, points and cries.

And voices were casting their shadows
On the road, or calling me. And my heart raced
As I turned around, to face the empty road.

V

Or, dans le même rêve
Je suis couché au plus creux d'une barque,
Le front, les yeux contre ses planches courbes
Où j'écoute cogner le bas du fleuve.
Et tout d'un coup cette proue se soulève,
J'imagine que là, déjà, c'est l'estuaire,
Mais je garde mes yeux contre le bois
Qui a odeur de goudron et de colle.
Trop vastes les images, trop lumineuses,
Que j'ai accumulées dans mon sommeil.
Pourquoi revoir, dehors,
Les choses dont les mots me parlent, mais sans convaincre,
Je désire plus haute ou moins sombre rive.

Et pourtant je renonce à ce sol qui bouge
Sous le corps qui se cherche, je me lève,
Je vais dans la maison de pièce en pièce,
Il y en a maintenant d'innombrables,
J'entends crier des voix derrière des portes,
Je suis saisi par ces douleurs qui cognent
Aux chambranles qui se délabrent, je me hâte,
Trop lourde m'est la nuit qui dure, j'entre effrayé
Dans une salle encombrée de pupitres,
Vois, me dit-on, ce fut ta salle de classe,
Vois sur les murs tes premières images,
Vois, c'est l'arbre, vois, là, c'est le chien qui jappe,
Et cette carte de géographie, sur la paroi

V

In the same dream
I lie in the hollow of a hull,
Eyes and forehead pressed to the curved planks
Where I can hear the river knocking.
Then suddenly the prow rides up. Already,
I imagine, this must be the river's mouth.
Even so I wedge my eyes against the wood
That smells of pitch and glue.
The images I've garnered in my sleep
Have been too vast, too luminous.
Why look outside again, why see the things
Words say to me, though unconvincingly,
When I desire a higher or less somber shore.

But I renounce this floor that moves
Under my uncertain body. I get up,
I walk through the house from room to room,
And now the rooms are numberless.
I hear voices shouting behind the doors.
I'm distressed by these torments that pound
At the decrepit doorjambs. I hurry by.
The night drags on. Fear weighs me down.
I enter a room crowded with desks.
Look, I am told. This classroom was yours.
Look at the wall. Those were your first images.
Look, there's the tree, and there's the yelping dog.
And this map that yellows on the wall,

Jaune, ce décolorement des noms et des formes,
Ce dessaisissement des montagnes, des fleuves,
Par la blancheur qui transit le langage,
Vois, ce fut ton seul livre. L'Isis du plâtre
Du mur de cette salle, qui s'écaille,
N'a jamais eu, elle n'aura rien d'autre
À entrouvrir pour toi, refermer sur toi.

VI

Je m'éveillai, mais c'était en voyage,
Le train avait roulé toute la nuit,
Il allait maintenant vers de grands nuages
Debout là-bas, serrés, aube que déchirait
À des instants le lacet de la foudre.
Je regardais l'avènement du monde
Dans les buissons du remblai ; et soudain
Cet autre feu, en contrebas d'un champ
De pierres et de vignes. Le vent, la pluie
Rabattaient sa fumée contre le sol,
Mais une flamme rouge s'y redressait,
Prenant à pleines mains le bas du ciel.
Depuis quand brûlais-tu, feu des vignerons ?
Qui t'avait voulu là et pour qui sur terre ?

Après quoi il fit jour ; et le soleil
Jeta de toutes parts ses milliers de flèches
Dans le compartiment où des dormeurs

This slow discoloring of names and shapes,
These rivers, these mountains that disappear
In the whiteness invading language:
This was your only book. Isis—
The plaster wall peeling in this room—
Has never had, will never have
Anything else to open up to you
Or close to you again.

VI

I woke up, but we were traveling.
The train had lumbered through the night.
Now it rolled toward massive clouds
That loomed in a cluster up ahead.
From time to time, lightning's whip tore the dawn.
I watched the advent of the world
Through the brush of the embankment; and suddenly
This other fire below, in a field
Of stones and vines. Rain and wind
Stamped its smoke down to the ground,
But the reddish flame stood up again,
Seizing the whole lower sky in its hands.
Grape-growers' fire, how long had you burned?
Who wanted you there? For whom on this earth?

Then daylight broke. The sun
Shot its thousand arrows everywhere
In that compartment where sleepers' heads

La tête dodelinait encore, sur la dentelle
Des coussins de lainage bleu. Je ne dormais pas,
J'avais trop l'âge encore de l'espérance,
Je dédiais mes mots aux montagnes basses,
Que je voyais venir à travers les vitres.

VII

Je me souviens, c'était un matin, l'été,
La fenêtre était entrouverte, je m'approchais,
J'apercevais mon père au fond du jardin.
Il était immobile, il regardait
Où, quoi, je ne savais, au-dehors de tout,
Voûté comme il était déjà mais redressant
Son regard vers l'inaccompli ou l'impossible.
Il avait déposé la pioche, la bêche,
L'air était frais ce matin-là du monde,
Mais impénétrable est la fraîcheur même, et cruel
Le souvenir des matins de l'enfance.
Qui était-il, qui avait-il été dans la lumière,
Je ne le savais pas, je ne sais encore.

Mais je le vois aussi, sur le boulevard,
Avançant lentement, tant de fatigue
Alourdissant ses gestes d'autrefois,
Il repartait au travail, quant à moi
J'errais avec quelques-uns de ma classe

Still nodded, on the lace of blue wool cushions.
But I was not sleeping. I still
Lived too deep in the age of hope.
I devoted my words to low mountains
I saw coming through the windows.

VII

I remember, it was a summer morning.
The window was half-open. As I came closer,
I saw my father there in the garden.
He stood motionless. Where he was looking,
Or at what, I could not tell—outside everything.
Stooped as he already was, he lifted his gaze
Toward the unachieved, or the impossible.
He had laid down the pickaxe, the spade.
The air was cool on that morning of the world.
But coolness is impenetrable, and cruel
Are the memories of childhood mornings.
Who he was, who he had been in the light:
I did not know, I still do not know.

But I also see him on the boulevard
Slowly walking forward, so much tiredness
Weighing down his gestures of former days.
He was going back to work. As for me,
I was strolling with some classmates

Au début de l'après-midi sans durée encore.
À ce passage-là, aperçu de loin,
Soient dédiés les mots qui ne savent dire.

(Dans la salle à manger
De l'après-midi d'un dimanche, c'est en été,
Les volets sont fermés contre la chaleur,
La table débarrassée, il a proposé
Les cartes puisqu'il n'est pas d'autres images
Dans la maison natale pour recevoir
La demande du rêve, puis il sort
Et aussitôt l'enfant maladroit prend les cartes,
Il substitue à celles de l'autre jeu
Toutes les cartes gagnantes, puis il attend
Avec fièvre, que la partie reprenne, et que celui
Qui perdait gagne, et si glorieusement
Qu'il y voie comme un signe, et de quoi nourrir
Il ne sait, lui l'enfant, quelle espérance.
Après quoi deux voies se séparent, et l'une d'elles
Se perd, et presque tout de suite, et ce sera
Tout de même l'oubli, l'oubli avide.

J'aurai barré
Cent fois ces mots partout, en vers, en prose,
Mais je ne puis
Faire qu'ils ne remontent dans ma parole.)

In the early afternoon, timeless as yet.
To his passing by, observed from afar, let me
Dedicate these words that don't know how to say.

(In the dining room
on a Sunday afternoon; it's summer.
The shutters are closed against the heat.
The table cleared, he proposes a game of cards.
In the house where I was born
There are no other images to still
The demands of dream. Later he steps out,
And the awkward child takes up the cards;
He replaces the ones that had been dealt
With a winning hand, then waits with bated breath
For the game to begin again. Now the loser would win,
So gloriously that he sees it
As something of a sign, something that might nourish—
What, being just a child, he cannot know—some kind of hope.
But after this their paths diverge. One of them
Is lost, almost right away. And forgetfulness,
Forgetfulness devours all.

I have crossed these words out everywhere
A hundred times, in verse, in prose,
But I cannot: always they well up again,
And tell their truth.)

VIII

J'ouvre les yeux, c'est bien la maison natale,
Et même celle qui fut et rien de plus.
La même petite salle à manger dont la fenêtre
Donne sur un pêcher qui ne grandit pas.
Un homme et une femme se sont assis
Devant cette croisée, l'un face à l'autre,
Ils se parlent, pour une fois. L'enfant
Du fond de ce jardin les voit, les regarde.
Il sait que l'on peut naître de ces mots.
Derrière les parents la salle est sombre.
L'homme vient de rentrer du travail. La fatigue
Qui a été le seul nimbe des gestes
Qu'il fut donné à son fils d'entrevoir
Le détache déjà de cette rive.

IX

Et alors un jour vint
Où j'entendis ce vers extraordinaire de Keats,
L'évocation de Ruth « when, sick for home,
She stood in tears amid the alien corn ».

Or, de ces mots
Je n'avais pas à pénétrer le sens
Car il était en moi depuis l'enfance,

VIII

I open my eyes:
This is the house where I was born,
Surely the one that was and nothing more.
The same small dining room looks out
On a peach tree that never grows.
A man and a woman have sat down
In front of the window, face to face.
They talk to each other for once. The child
Sees them from the garden: he watches them,
Knowing that life can be born from these words.
Behind his parents the room is dark.
The man has just returned from work. Fatigue,
The only nimbus of his gestures
Ever granted his son to glimpse,
Detaches him already from this shore.

IX

Then came the day that I first heard
The extraordinary verse of Keats,
Evoking Ruth "when, sick for home,
She stood in tears amid the alien corn."

I did not have to grapple
With the meaning of these words,
Since it was in me from my childhood.

Je n'ai eu qu'à le reconnaître, et à l'aimer
Quand il est revenu du fond de ma vie.

Qu'avais-je eu, en effet, à recueillir
De l'évasive présence maternelle
Sinon le sentiment de l'exil et les larmes
Qui troublaient ce regard cherchant à voir
Dans les choses d'ici le lieu perdu ?

X

La vie, alors ; et ce fut à nouveau
Une maison natale. Autour de nous
Le grenier d'au-dessus l'église défaite,
Le jeu d'ombres léger des nuées de l'aube,
Et en nous cette odeur de la paille sèche
Restée à nous attendre, nous semblait-il,
Depuis le dernier sac monté, de blé ou seigle,
Dans l'autrefois sans fin de la lumière
Des étés tamisés par les tuiles chaudes.
Je pressentais que le jour allait poindre,
Je m'éveillais, et je me tourne encore
Vers celle qui rêva à côté de moi
Dans la maison perdue. À son silence
Soient dédiés, au soir,
Les mots qui semblent ne parler que d'autre chose.

I only needed to recognize and love
What had returned from the depths of my life.

And truly, what could I have gleaned
From that evasive mother's presence
If not the sense of exile? Tears
Clouding her eyes that tried to see
A long-lost place in the here and now.

X

Life, then: and once again
A house where I was born. The granary
Above a ruined church enfolded us.
Pale clouds shadow-played at dawn.
It seemed this odor of dry straw
Had waited to pervade us—ever since
They stored the last sack of wheat or rye
In those unended days of bygone radiance,
Of summers filtering through sun-warmed tiles.
I sensed that dawn was going to break,
That soon I would wake up. And now I turn again
To her who dreamed beside me
In the house we have lost. This evening,
To her silence, let me dedicate these words
That only seem to speak of something else.

(Je m'éveillais,
J'aimais ces jours que nous avions, jours préservés
Comme va lentement un fleuve, bien que déjà
Pris dans le bruit de voûtes de la mer.
Ils avançaient, avec la majesté des choses simples,
Les grandes voiles de ce qui est voulaient bien prendre
L'humaine vie précaire sur le navire
Qu'étendait la montagne autour de nous.
Ô souvenir,
Elles couvraient des claquements de leur silence
Le bruit, d'eau sur les pierres, de nos voix,
Et en avant ce serait bien la mort,
Mais de cette couleur laiteuse du bout des plages
Le soir, quand les enfants
Ont pied, loin, et rient dans l'eau calme, et jouent encore.)

XI

Et je repars, et c'est sur un chemin
Qui monte et tourne, bruyères, dunes
Au-dessus d'un bruit encore invisible, avec parfois
Le bien furtif du chardon bleu des sables.
Ici, le temps se creuse, c'est déjà
L'eau éternelle à bouger dans l'écume,
Je suis bientôt à deux pas du rivage.

(I was almost awake.
How I loved those days of ours, preserved
The way a river slows, already caught
In the resounding arches of the sea.
They moved with the majesty of simple things.
Vast sails, the sails of all that is, agreed to lift
Our fragile human life aboard the ship
That the mountains wrapped around us.
O memory,
Their luffing silence decked the sound
Our voices made, like water on stones.
No doubt on the horizon would be death:
But milky as that shade where beaches end,
At evening, when the children still touch bottom
Far into the sea, laughing in tranquil waters, and still play.)

XI

And I start out again, along a path
That climbs and turns. Moors and dunes,
Above a sound as yet invisible. In the sand,
Now and then, blue thistle's furtive gift.
Time goes hollow here, becomes
Eternal water surging in the foam.
And soon I stand two steps from the sea.

Et je vois qu'un navire attend au large,
Noir, tel un candélabre à nombre de branches
Qu'enveloppent des flammes et des fumées.
Qu'allons-nous faire ? crie-t-on de toutes parts,
Ne faut-il pas aider ceux qui là-bas
Nous demandent rivage ? Oui, clame l'ombre,
Et je vois des nageurs qui, dans la nuit,
Se portent vers le navire, soutenant
D'une main au-dessus de l'eau agitée,
Des lampes, aux longues banderoles de couleur.
La beauté même, en son lieu de naissance,
Quand elle n'est encore que vérité.

XII

Beauté et vérité, mais ces hautes vagues
Sur ces cris qui s'obstinent. Comment garder
Audible l'espérance dans le tumulte,
Comment faire pour que vieillir, ce soit renaître,
Pour que la maison s'ouvre, de l'intérieur,
Pour que ce ne soit pas que la mort qui pousse
Dehors celui qui demandait un lieu natal ?

Je comprends maintenant que ce fût Cérès
Qui me parut, de nuit, chercher refuge
Quand on frappait à la porte, et dehors,
C'était d'un coup sa beauté, sa lumière

I discover that a ship waits offshore:
A black candelabra, all its boughs
Engulfed in flames and smoke.
What can we do? people cry out on every side.
Shouldn't we help the voyagers out there
Who're asking us for berth? Yes, darkness shouts.
And then I see how swimmers in the night
Race toward the ship with one hand raised
Above the stormy swells, holding lamps
That stream with colored pennants.
Beauty itself in its place of birth,
When not yet anything but truth.

XII

Beauty and truth. But tall waves crash
On cries that still persist. The voice of hope,
Above the din—how can we make it heard?
How can growing old become rebirth?
How can the house be opened from within,
So death will not turn out the child
Who asked for a native place?

Now I understand: it was Ceres
Who sought shelter on the night
Someone was knocking at the door.
Outside, her beauty suddenly flared—
Her light and her desire too, her need

Et son désir aussi, son besoin de boire
Avidement au bol de l'espérance
Parce qu'était perdu mais retrouvable
Peut-être, cet enfant qu'elle n'avait su,
Elle pourtant divine et riche de soi,
Soulever dans la flamme des jeunes blés
Pour qu'il ait rire, dans l'évidence qui fait vivre
Avant la convoitise du dieu des morts.

Et pitié pour Cérès et non moquerie,
Rendez-vous à des carrefours dans la nuit profonde,
Cris d'appels au travers des mots, même sans réponse,
Parole même obscure mais qui puisse
Aimer enfin Cérès qui cherche et souffre.

To slake her thirst with the cup of hope:
She might still find that child again,
Even if lost. Though rich with herself,
Rich with her divinity, she had not known
How to lift her child in the young wheat's flame,
Laughing in the simple light that gives us life—
Before the god of the dead, and all his greed.

We must pity Ceres, not mock her—and so
Must meet at crossroads in deepest night,
Call out athwart our words, even with no reply:
And make our voice, no matter how obscure,
Love Ceres at last, who suffers and seeks.

LES PLANCHES COURBES

L'homme était grand, très grand, qui se tenait sur la rive, près de la barque. La clarté de la lune était derrière lui, posée sur l'eau du fleuve. À un léger bruit l'enfant qui s'approchait, lui tout à fait silencieusement, comprenait que la barque bougeait, contre son appontement ou une pierre. Il tenait serrée dans sa main la petite pièce de cuivre.

« Bonjour, monsieur », dit-il d'une voix claire mais qui tremblait parce qu'il craignait d'attirer trop fort l'attention de l'homme, du géant, qui était là immobile. Mais le passeur, absent de soi comme il semblait l'être, l'avait déjà aperçu, sous les roseaux. « Bonjour, mon petit, répondit-il. Qui es-tu ?

— Oh, je ne sais pas, dit l'enfant.

— Comment, tu ne sais pas ! Est-ce que tu n'as pas de nom ? »

L'enfant essaya de comprendre ce que pouvait être un nom. « Je ne sais pas », dit-il à nouveau, assez vite.

« Tu ne sais pas ! Mais tu sais bien ce que tu entends quand on te fait signe, quand on t'appelle ?

— On ne m'appelle pas.

— On ne t'appelle pas quand il faut rentrer à la maison ? Quand tu as joué dehors et que c'est l'heure pour ton repas, pour dormir ? N'as-tu pas un père, une mère ? Où est ta maison, dis-moi. »

Et l'enfant de se demander maintenant ce que c'est qu'un père, une mère ; ou une maison.

« Un père, dit-il, qu'est-ce que c'est ? »

Le passeur s'assit sur une pierre, près de sa barque. Sa voix vint de moins loin dans la nuit. Mais il avait eu d'abord une sorte de petit rire.

« Un père? Eh bien, celui qui te prend sur ses genoux quand tu

THE CURVED PLANKS

The man who stood on the bank near the boat was tall, very tall. Behind him moonlight nestled on the waters. As the boy approached the river in utter silence, he heard faint thumps: he knew the boat must be bumping gently against the dock, or a stone. He held the small copper coin clutched tight in his hand.

"Hello, Sir," he said in a clear voice, though it trembled. He feared he was making himself too obtrusive to the ferryman. The giant loomed there, motionless. He seemed to be distracted; yet he had already noticed the child, under the reeds. "Hello, my boy," he replied. "Who are you?"

"Oh, I don't know," said the child.

"What, you don't know! Don't you have a name?"

The child tried to grasp what a name might be. "I don't know," he said again, quickly enough.

"You don't know! But you have to know what you hear when somebody waves at you or calls!"

"Nobody calls me."

"Nobody calls you when it's time to come home? When you've been playing outside and it's mealtime, or bedtime? Don't you have a father, a mother? Where is your home? Tell me."

Now the boy was wondering what a father might be, or a mother, or a home.

"A father," he said. "What's that?"

The ferryman sat down on a stone near his boat. Though at first he'd laughed a bit, now his voice came from less far away in the night.

"A father? Well, he's the one who takes you on his knees when you

pleures, et qui s'assied près de toi le soir lorsque tu as peur de t'endormir, pour te raconter une histoire. »

L'enfant ne répondit pas.

« Souvent on n'a pas eu de père, c'est vrai, reprit le géant comme après quelque réflexion. Mais alors il y a ces jeunes et douces femmes, dit-on, qui allument le feu, qui vous assoient près de lui, qui vous chantent une chanson. Et quand elles s'éloignent, c'est pour faire cuire des plats, on sent l'odeur de l'huile qui chauffe dans la marmite.

— Je ne me souviens pas de cela non plus », dit l'enfant de sa légère voix cristalline. Il s'était approché du passeur qui maintenant se taisait, il entendait sa respiration égale, lente. « Je dois passer le fleuve, dit-il. J'ai de quoi payer le passage. »

Le géant se pencha, le prit dans ses vastes mains, le plaça sur ses épaules, se redressa et descendit dans sa barque, qui céda un peu sous son poids. « Allons, dit-il. Tiens-toi bien fort à mon cou ! » D'une main, il retenait l'enfant par une jambe, de l'autre il planta la perche dans l'eau. L'enfant se cramponna à son cou d'un mouvement brusque, avec un soupir. Le passeur put prendre alors la perche à deux mains, il la retira de la boue, la barque quitta la rive, le bruit de l'eau s'élargit sous les reflets, dans les ombres.

Et un instant après un doigt toucha son oreille. « Écoute, dit l'enfant, veux-tu être mon père ? » Mais il s'interrompit aussitôt, la voix brisée par les larmes.

« Ton père ! Mais je ne suis que le passeur ! Je ne m'éloigne jamais d'un bord ou de l'autre du fleuve.

— Mais je resterais avec toi, au bord du fleuve.

cry, who sits down beside you in the evening when you're afraid to go to sleep and tells you a story."

The boy didn't answer.

"True, often children haven't had a father," the giant went on, as though reconsidering. "But then, they say, there are sweet young women who light the fire so you can sit down close to it, and who sing you a song. If they go away awhile it's only to cook some food; you can smell the oil heating in the pan."

"I don't remember that either," said the boy in his light, crystal voice. He had drawn closer to the ferryman, who now fell silent; he could hear his breathing, slow and even. "I need to cross the river," he said. "I have enough to pay the fare."

The giant bent down and scooped him up in his enormous hands. After setting him on his shoulders, he stood up and climbed down into the boat. It gave way a little under his weight. "All right, let's go," he said. "Hang on tight to my neck!" With one hand he gripped the child by a leg, and with the other he stuck the pole in the water. In a sudden movement, the boy embraced the ferryman's neck, and let out a sigh. Now the giant was able to grasp the pole with both hands; he pulled it out of the mud, and the boat slipped away from the shore. The water rushed more loudly under the glimmering, in the shadows.

A moment later a finger touched his ear. "Listen," said the child, "do you want to be my father?" But he broke off right away, his voice choked by tears.

"Your father! Why, I'm only the ferryman! I never stray far from the riverbank."

"But I would stay with you here, along the river."

— Pour être un père, il faut avoir une maison, ne comprends-tu pas ? Je n'ai pas de maison, je vis dans les joncs de la rive.

— Je resterais si volontiers auprès de toi sur la rive !

— Non, dit le passeur, ce n'est pas possible. Et vois, d'ailleurs ! »

Ce qu'il faut voir, c'est que la barque semble fléchir de plus en plus sous le poids de l'homme et de l'enfant, qui s'accroît à chaque seconde. Le passeur peine à la pousser en avant, l'eau arrive à hauteur du bord, elle le franchit, elle emplit la coque de ses courants, elle atteint le haut de ces grandes jambes qui sentent se dérober tout appui dans les planches courbes. L'esquif ne coule pas, cependant, c'est plutôt comme s'il dissipait, dans la nuit, et l'homme nage, maintenant, le petit garçon toujours agrippé a son cou. « N'aie pas peur, dit-il, le fleuve n'est pas si large, nous arriverons bientôt.

— Oh, s'il te plaît, sois mon père ! Sois ma maison !

— Il faut oublier tout cela, répond le géant, a voix basse. Il faut oublier ces mots. Il faut oublier les mots. »

Il a repris dans sa main la petite jambe, qui est immense déjà, et de son bras libre il nage dans cet espace sans fin de courants qui s'entrechoquent, d'abîmes qui s'entrouvrent, d'étoiles.

"To be a father, you have to have a home, don't you understand? I don't have one. I live in the rushes along the bank."

"I'd be so glad to stay near you, along the bank!"

"No," said the ferryman, "it isn't possible. And anyway, look!"

What must be seen is this: the boat seems to sink more and more beneath the man and the child, whose weight keeps increasing by the second. The ferryman labors to push the skiff forward, as water keeps pouring in over the sides. Currents swirl through the hull, reaching the giant's thighs. In his huge legs he senses that the curved planks are giving way. Even so the boat does not founder; instead it seems to melt into the night. The man is swimming now, with the little boy still clinging to his neck. "Don't be afraid," he says. "The river isn't very wide. We'll get there soon."

"Oh please, be my father! Be my home!"

"You have to forget all that," the giant answers under his breath. "You have to forget those words. You have to forget all words."

He clasps the small leg—immense already—in his hand again, and with his free arm he swims in the limitless space of clashing currents, of yawning abysses, of stars.

FROM DANS UN DÉBRIS DE MIROIR

IN A SHARD OF MIRROR

TROIS SOUVENIRS DE BORGES

I

Je tourne dans ma mémoire les pages d'un de mes livres de souvenirs. Celui-ci, quelques images d'un homme qui me donna d'emblée l'impression qu'il y avait en lui une souffrance aussi profonde qu'ancienne dans sa vie, mais par pudeur gardée tue.

Trois souvenirs, et d'abord celui de la première rencontre. C'était à Cambridge, Massachusetts, en 1967. Borges venait d'arriver en ville pour donner les Charles Eliot Norton Lectures à Harvard durant l'hiver. Je l'admirais, je savais que j'aimerais l'homme que je pressentais qu'il était, je disais cela à Jorge Guillén, qui vivait à Cambridge lui aussi, et que je voyais souvent, soit seul, soit avec Paul de Man, alors à des déjeuners. Jorge me dit : « Borges est là, il s'installe, écrivez-lui, demandez-lui rendez-vous ».

J'écrivis mais une dizaine de jours se passèrent sans m'apporter de réponse. Après quoi Guillén me dit, en riant : « Savez-vous ? Je suis passé chez Borges, hier après-midi. Elsa m'a pris à part pour me demander à voix basse, Connaissez-vous cette femme ? Elle tenait votre lettre, et à cause de votre prénom, que Borges avait prononcé à voix haute, elle a conclu qu'il lui fallait empêcher cette rencontre ».

Mon prénom ? Il se prononce comme en anglais celui d'Ève, du simple fait de laquelle tout dans le monde aurait mal tourné. La femme de Borges, elle, était une nouveauté. Sa mère la lui avait imposée, disait-on, quand elle s'était sentie trop âgée pour l'accompagner en voyage. Est-ce vrai, en tout cas Elsa ne resta que très peu d'années dans sa vie. On ne pouvait imaginer deux êtres plus dif-

THREE RECOLLECTIONS OF BORGES

I

In my memory, I turn the pages of one of my keepsake books. It holds some images of a man whose life hinged on a suffering, old and profound, which his quiet reserve never allowed him to mention. That was my impression of him, right from the start.

Three recollections, beginning with our first encounter: in Cambridge, Massachusetts, in 1967. Borges was slated to give the Charles Eliot Norton Lectures at Harvard that winter. I admired him, convinced I'd like the man I guessed he must be. Jorge Guillén was living in Cambridge, too, and I saw him often—either alone, or for lunch with Paul de Man. When I spoke to him of Borges, Jorge said: "He's here already, settling in. Write him, and ask if you could meet."

I wrote him; but ten days went by, and still no reply. At last, Guillén reported to me with a laugh: "Guess what? I called on Borges yesterday, and Elsa took me aside. "Do you know this woman?" she asked, in a low voice. "She had your letter in her hand. Borges had said your first name out loud, so she decided to keep him from seeing you."

My first name? It's pronounced like the English name, "Eve"—a temptress who fouled up everything on earth, reputedly. That Borges should have a wife was a novelty: it was rumored his mother had forced her on him, when she'd grown too old to travel with him herself. True or false, Elsa only shared his existence for very few years. It would be hard to imagine two beings more dissimilar; and the

férents et les vieux amis de Borges, il y en avait plusieurs à Cambridge, en étaient déconcertés, malheureux.

« Vous vous trompez, répondit Guillén. Ce n'est pas une femme, et c'est un ami. Il n'est pas dangereux pour vous, laissez Borges lui répondre ».

Borges téléphona, un soir. Il acceptait de venir dîner chez nous, Francis Avenue. Cette fois-là, qui dura un an, nous avions loué une petite maison de bois attenante à une plus grande qui avait, elle, pignon sur rue au-dessus de quatre ou cinq marches entre deux colonnes de bois. Et nous nous étions épris de ce lieu, modestement exemplaire de cette façon d'être au monde, frémissements des planchers, vitres tout contre les arbres, qui voue qui s'en va de la Nouvelle-Angleterre à une nostalgie qui sera sans fin. Nous faisions des feux dans la cheminée et tantôt c'était le printemps, avec beaucoup de branches et feuilles de toutes parts, tantôt l'automne et toutes ces feuilles se faisaient alors du rouge et de l'or puis tombaient, à foison, nous avancions dans le léger bruit qu'elles faisaient sous nos pas. Et bientôt ou déjà c'était aussi de la neige. Il avait neigé le jour où vinrent dîner « les Borges ».

Je ne l'avais jamais rencontré avant. Et tout de suite ou presque, avec cette confiance qu'il avait, de toujours, semble-t-il, décidé de faire à ceux qui venaient à lui, il expliqua qu'il arrivait de Concord, où il avait voulu visiter la maison de Hawthorne. Il admirait immensément Nathaniel Hawthorne. Et c'était donc un jour de grand froid, de beaucoup de neige, mais par dévotion pour ce grand écrivain, peut-être aussi par attrait pour la vie que celui-ci avait menée là, dans une communauté occupée d'une foi que lui, Borges, n'avait certes plus, il

author's old friends, several of whom resided in Cambridge, felt unhappy and disconcerted about her role.

"You're mistaken," Guillén informed her. "He's not a woman; and he happens to be a friend of mine. He's no threat to you. So please let Borges answer him."

One evening, Borges phoned me; he agreed to come to dinner at our house on Francis Avenue. For that stay, which lasted about a year, my wife and I had rented a small frame house; it adjoined a larger one, raised by four or five steps, that surveyed the street between two wooden columns. We'd fallen in love with the creaking floors, and the windowpanes flush against the trees. This modest place exemplified a way of being in the world—which is why those who leave New England feel such a homesickness, ever after. We laid fires in the chimney: now it was spring, with leafy branches on every side; and now it was autumn. Then all those leaves turned red and gold before they fell, in such profusion they crackled softly under our feet. And soon enough, there was snow; it had snowed the day "the Borgeses" came to dinner.

Even though I'd never met him before, he conversed with me openly right away—he always placed that trust in those who sought him out, I gathered. He'd just returned from Concord, he explained. He'd been eager to visit Hawthorne's house, since he revered him enormously. Out of devotion to this great writer, he'd knelt on the doorstep, despite the bitter cold and heavy snow. Perhaps he'd done so in part because of the life Hawthorne had led there, in a community

s'était agenouillé sur le perron, dans cette neige. Puis il me dit, avez-vous lu « Wakefield » ?

Je n'avais pas lu « Wakefield », et Borges entreprit de résumer ce récit. Un homme dit à sa femme qu'il va s'absenter pour un jour ou deux. Il part avec un « sourire idiot ». Mais quelques rues plus loin, il s'arrête. Pourquoi irais-je ailleurs, se demande-t-il ? Il prend dans un hôtel une chambre en attendant que ce soit demain, et rentrer chez lui.

Mais le lendemain : pourquoi rentrerais-je aujourd'hui ? Wakefield remet de le faire pendant des jours, des mois, des années. C'est pourtant tout près de sa maison qu'il est resté, on pourrait dire à deux pas. Vaguement déguisé, il passe souvent devant elle. De temps en temps, précise Borges, il aperçoit, de loin, sa femme dans une rue, vieillissante. Il ne fait rien, cependant, tout au long de ces vingt ans, ne fréquente personne, ne comprend rien.

Et voici qu'un jour il est dans sa rue, et il pleut, une rafale le pousse contre sa porte, pourquoi ne pas rentrer, se dit-il. Il sonne, il rentre, il reprend sa vie d'autrefois avec le même sourire idiot qu'il avait eu au moment de son départ.

Impressionnant ce récit, d'autant que Borges le rapporte avec une émotion bien visible. Dans cet hiver déjà rigoureux nous sommes dans une de ces maisons de l'époque de Hawthorne, il y a un feu dans la cheminée devant lequel la compagne du visiteur s'agenouille, un bouchon à la pointe d'un pique-feu parce qu'elle veut démontrer qu'on peut fabriquer du rimmel en carbonisant du liège. Et je me dis qu'une des raisons de l'attrait que Borges éprouve si fort pour les États-Unis a partie liée aux maisons de ce pays, à ce qu'elles offraient à Hawthorne d'austère confort pour réfléchir à Dieu, à la société, à sa

imbued by faith—though a faith Borges himself certainly didn't profess. Then he asked me: "Have you ever read 'Wakefield'?"

Since I hadn't read "Wakefield," Borges summarized the tale for me in French. A man tells his wife he's going out of town for a day or two. He takes leave of her with a "sourire idiot"—a "stupid smile." But a few streets away, he stops. Why travel any further? he shrugs. He takes a room in a nearby hotel, planning to go back home the next day.

But the next morning, Wakefield thinks: why should I go home right now? And so he postpones his return for days, months, years. All this time, he remains very near his house—just a stone's throw away, so to speak. Vaguely disguised, he often strolls in front of it. Now and then, from a distance, he catches sight of his wife on the street; he can see she's growing old, Borges noted. Still, it's not that Wakefield is up to anything unusual; for twenty years, he doesn't see a soul, and doesn't have a clue.

Then one day, he's walking down the street again. It's raining, and a gust of wind happens to push him against his door. Why not step inside? he says to himself. He rings the bell, goes in, and takes up his former life, with the same "stupid smile" as when he left, many years before.

The story made its mark, especially since Borges was visibly moved as he recounted it. The winter, already severe, found us sheltered by a house from Hawthorne's time, as well. Our guest's companion was kneeling on the hearth before the fire, with a wine-stopper stuck to the end of a poker; she wanted to prove you could make mascara by charring cork. I think one thing that drew Borges so strongly to the United States was the houses of that country. They'd offered an austere comfort to Hawthorne, so he could ponder God, society, and his

propre vie : ce qui déjà explique qu'il ait pensé à « Wakefield », ce soir, à son retour de Concord. Mais ce « sourire idiot », ces mots qu'il a répétés avec même quelque emphase ? L'adjectif étonne, par sa violence, dans le contexte de ce récit qui semble tout en nuances et je me demande quel est le mot anglais qu'a traduit de cette façon ce lecteur averti, et qui sait le français si bien.

Le lendemain j'ai lu « Wakefield », et je le relis aujourd'hui. Le sourire de Wakefield est chez Hawthorne aussi le centre de la réflexion. Il le voit, et par les yeux aussi de l'épouse qui se croit veuve, quand celle-ci se remémore ce départ soudain, imprévu, et tente 'même, pour le comprendre, de placer ce sourire étrange sur les traits de son mari mort, sur un visage figé. Mais le mot qu'emploie Hawthorne n'est nullement l'équivalent du français « idiot », il parle d'un « *crafty* smile ».

« Crafty », un bel et riche adjectif dont, tout à l'opposé du français « idiot », l'idée d'intelligence n'est pas absente, ni celle de l'habileté, de la maîtrise lucide d'une pratique au moyen de techniques souvent précises ; mais qui a pris à travers les siècles et de façon irrésistible et irréversible un tour nettement péjoratif. Le substantif associable à cet adjectif, « craft », échappant toutefois à ce jugement, dans une certaine mesure. Comme si on sentait, instinctivement, que reste dans la maîtrise d'un faire un possible libérateur, dans ce mal en puissance la prémonition d'un vrai bien. En bref, dans « crafty » peut fort bien s'inscrire la hantise du mal d'un christianisme débarqué du *Mayflower* avec sur le dos tout un faix de peurs archaïques. Tandis que dans « craft » se préservent les intuitions et les équilibres de certains travaux, souvent de nature artisanale, qui sont au cœur de la société.

Je constatai donc que lorsque Borges disait « idiot » il avait « crafty »

own existence. This may be why Borges thought of "Wakefield" that evening, on his return from Concord. But what of the "sourire idiot"? He'd repeated the words, with an emphatic flourish. The adjective sounded oddly harsh, in a narrative that seemed so nuanced. I wondered what English term this accomplished reader had translated there, since he knew his French so well.

The next day I read "Wakefield," and I've reread it again today. In Hawthorne, too, Wakefield's smile is the touchstone of the tale. At one point, he depicts it through the eyes of the character's wife—who believes she's a widow—as she recalls her husband's sudden, unexpected departure. To grasp that strange smile, she even tries to impose it on his death-locked features, his rigid face. But the word used by Hawthorne isn't at all the English twin of the French modifier, "idiot"; in fact, he speaks of a "*crafty* smile."

"Crafty" is a rich and beautiful adjective. As opposed to the French "idiot," it conveys the idea of a certain intelligence, a cleverness, the lucid mastery of techniques that are often quite precise; but over the centuries, irresistibly and irreversibly, the term has acquired a pejorative stamp. Even so, the related substantive, "craft," has largely escaped that connotation. It's as if we sensed, instinctively, that in the mastery of a practice, we might attain our freedom: that through a potential evil, we might achieve a genuine good. To sum up, "crafty" reflects the evil-obsessed Christianity brought over on the *Mayflower,* freighted with archaic fears; whereas "craft" preserves the even-keeled know-how of specific trades—often handicrafts—that lie at the heart of society.

So I inferred that when Borges said "idiot" in French, he must have

en esprit. « Idiot », un mot qui constate plutôt qu'il ne condamne, comme si le traducteur improvisé voulait excuser Wakefield, éprouvant à son égard autant de compassion que de fascination.

Et je ne pus faire moins que me souvenir que les Norton Lectures que Borges s'apprêtait à donner à Harvard, ce lieu de toutes les sophistications, avaient pour titre *This Craft of Verse*, un titre que je n'avais pu que trouver provocateur par le déport qu'à l'encontre de toute une tradition il suggérait dans la pensée de la poésie : de l'idée de celle-ci comme occasion, ou cause, d'expérience spirituelle passant à celle du poème comme production, montage de figures, objet verbal à confier aux soins pourtant spécieux d'une rhétorique.

Les conférences eurent lieu, qui ont attiré, au moins la première, tout ce qu'il y avait d'intellect le long de la côte est des États-Unis depuis New York, ou même au-delà. La notoriété de Borges était alors à son comble, après quelques années d'un curieux retard. Mais dans cette attention il y avait l'idée d'un auteur extrêmement subtil, voire alambiqué, et grande fut la surprise des auditeurs. Ai-je rêvé cette conférence ? Assurément je vais la déformer, la trahir, on va s'inscrire en faux contre moi, mais je ne puis effacer de mon esprit l'impression que me firent ses premiers mots. Borges parlait sans notes, il ne pouvait en avoir. Il parla d'ailleurs peu longtemps, prenant parfois sur la table une grosse montre qu'il faisait passer sous ses yeux, de vraiment très près. Et il s'exprima avec ce qui me parut, à moi en tout cas, une simplicité elle encore très provocante. Les Chinois constatent qu'il y a mille mots, dit-il. À cela il n'y a pas grand chose à ajouter. Peut-être seulement qu'il y a dix métaphores.

Sur quoi il énuméra les dix métaphores, par exemple, le temps, c'est un fleuve qui coule, ou la bataille, c'est un brasier. Ah, peut-être y

had "crafty" in mind. "Stupid" is a word that comments, rather than condemns: the unguarded translator had wanted to excuse Wakefield —as though he felt compassion for him, along with fascination.

I couldn't help recalling that the Norton Lectures Borges was about to deliver at Harvard—that Mecca of sophistication—bore the title: *This Craft of Verse*. I found the title provocative, since it seemed to defy a whole tradition of thought: that poetry could be the occasion, or the cause, of a spiritual experience. Instead, it implied the poem was just a product, a montage of figures—a verbal object we could entrust to rhetoric, however bogus its devices.

The lectures duly took place, and the first one, at least, convened the leading minds of the entire East Coast—from as far away as New York, and beyond. The notoriety of Borges was then at its height, after several years of unaccountable delay. But it rested on an image of the author as highly subtle, even convoluted, and many of the listeners were taken aback by his talk. Is my remembrance of it just a dream? No doubt I'm about to distort his lecture, even betray it; people will complain that I'm mistaken. Still, I can't erase the impression made on me by his first remarks. Borges spoke without notes, since he couldn't use them. In fact, he didn't go on for long: from time to time, he picked up a large watch from the table, holding it close to his eyes. Once again, he expressed himself with what appeared—to me, anyway—like a simplicity meant to provoke. "The Chinese have observed there are only a thousand words," he said. "After that, there's not much to add. Maybe just this: that there are ten metaphors."

Then he counted off the ten metaphors. For example, time is a flowing river, or battle is an inferno. "Oh, maybe there's another meta-

a-t-il une autre métaphore digne d'attention, ajouta-t-il à la fin, celle qu'un poète américain, E. E. Cummings, a risquée : « The face of God is shining like a spoon ». Mais à la réflexion, non, ce n'est pas à ajouter à la liste, conclut-il.

Ai-je moi aussi simplifié, en tout cas l'étonnement était grand chez quelques-uns au moins, à la fin de la conférence. Je retrouvai Borges dans le couloir. « Que faites-vous donc de Mallarmé ? lui ai-je demandé. — Ah, Mallarmé, c'est trop compliqué. — Mais Baudelaire, alors ? — Baudelaire ? C'est un orgueilleux », me répondit-il très sérieusement.

Il aimait répéter que le meilleur de la poésie française, c'était bien moins les quelques poètes dont nous faisons notre modernité, méditant leur pensée sur la poésie et son rôle dans la conscience de soi, que Verlaine ou même Paul-Jean Toulet, pour lequel il éprouvait une tendresse particulière. Et bien facile à comprendre était ce refus, qu'il étendait à beaucoup des façons d'être et des valeurs qu'il imaginait notre habitude française. La poésie se doit à ce qui importe, c'est-à-dire à la compassion et à l'humilité qui en est une des conséquences. Ceux qui la veulent à plus haut niveau dans l'esprit sont des orgueilleux, qui ne veulent pas reconnaître les étroites limites du fait humain, et cette démesure en fera la proie du mal, qui aura chance de triompher par leur truchement. Mieux aurait donc valu pour eux de n'être que des idiots, comme ce Wakefield, il aurait été plus aisé d'éprouver à leur égard la compassion que chacun mérite, sur la vaine scène du monde.

Je crois fondée cette sorte de critique, elle est même ce qui m'attirait chez Borges. À mon sens elle fait la grandeur d'un écrivain que l'on a dit souvent sans capacité d'amour, alors qu'à l'évidence il était

phor worth our while," he threw in at the end. "An American poet, E. E. Cummings, has dared to write: 'The face of God is shining like a spoon.'" But on further reflection, he concluded: "No, that one shouldn't be admitted to the list."

I may have oversimplified, in turn; but at any rate, some of his listeners were more than a little nonplussed, when the lecture came to halt. I met up with Borges afterwards in the hallway. "What do you make of Mallarmé, then?" I asked him. "Oh, Mallarmé—he's too complicated." "Then how about Baudelaire?" "Baudelaire? He's too arrogant," he replied, in all earnestness.

They belong to that handful of poets we've acknowledged in France as the source of our modernity: we often contemplate their thoughts on poetry, and its role in our awareness of the self. But Borges liked to claim their work wasn't the best of French verse; he preferred Verlaine, or even Paul-Jean Toulet, for whom he felt a special fondness. This rebuff of his—which he extended to many attitudes and values he conceived of as French—was easily understandable. Poetry owes a debt to what's truly important: compassion, and the humility that it instills. Those who want to raise poetry to some loftier plane of the mind are arrogant: they refuse to accept the narrow limits of the human condition. Their excesses make poetry fall prey to evil, which may win out because of their meddling. They'd be better off just being stupid, like Wakefield; then we could more readily show them the indulgence each of us deserves, on the vain stage of this world.

I believe that kind of criticism is well-founded; indeed, it's what appealed to me in Borges. In my view, it underpins the grandeur of a writer who's often been taxed as incapable of love. On the contrary, he was ravaged by the pain and mortality of those around him, appalled

ravagé par la pensée qu'autour de lui on était mortel, souffrant, et que du simple fait d'être soi on pouvait causer un tort irréparable à bien d'autres, comme d'ailleurs il l'a dit, explicitement et de façon saisissante, dans « Le jardin aux sentiers qui bifurquent ». La compassion, le sentiment d'impuissance qui en résulte, c'est bien ce qui causait chez Borges la souffrance qui paraissait dans sa façon d'être fondamentale, celle que j'ai évoquée aux premières lignes, et ce regard a droit de porter jugement, même ou surtout en littérature.

Mais une telle pensée ne vaut évidemment pas dans le cas de Mallarmé ou de Baudelaire, qui ne furent ni des compliqués ni des orgueilleux, ce que Borges savait d'ailleurs tout aussi bien que quiconque. Et son refus de ce soir-là et de si souvent ne visait, en fait, nullement ces deux grands poètes mais bien plutôt cet autre grand qu'il était lui-même, et qu'il craignait compliqué et ne voulait pas orgueilleux. Il considérait l'écriture comme une clôture de la personne sur soi, c'est-à-dire comme le meurtre d'autrui, et cela d'autant plus qu'était plus important l'écrivain. À travers Mallarmé ou Baudelaire, il s'inquiétait de soi, quitte à trouver dans leur évident surcroît sur ce jugement péremptoire de quoi se rassurer sur lui-même.

II

Un second souvenir, quelques années plus tard, 1974, au crépuscule de l'interminable guerre au Vietnam et au pire moment de Watergate. New York est obsédé par un sentiment d'insécurité, les rues la nuit sont désertes, rentrer cette nuit de New Haven sera ressentir quelque nervosité, même en attendant le taxi à proximité de Grand Central, toutefois beaucoup de jeunes gens, bien qu'ils ne soient plus les

that by merely being ourselves, we might inflict an irreparable hurt on our fellow men. He said as much, plainly and boldly, in "The Garden of Forking Paths." Compassion—and the sense of helplessness it entails—surely underlies the suffering I invoked from the outset as fundamental to Borges. This stance has every right to pass judgment, even—or above all—in literature.

But obviously, such strictures don't apply to either Mallarmé or Baudelaire; they weren't complicated or arrogant, and Borges knew this as well as anyone. His rejection of them that evening, as so often, didn't take aim at those great poets at all, but rather at the great man he was himself: he feared complication, and refused arrogance. He considered writing a person's walling in of the self—or in other words, the murder of everyone else—and all the more so, the more important the writer. Through Mallarmé and Baudelaire, he worried about his own dilemma; and since they clearly rose above such a grave indictment, he could feel reassured about himself.

II

A second recollection, from several years later: 1974. The nadir of Watergate; the interminable dusk of the war in Vietnam. A mood of insecurity haunted New York, and after dark the streets lay deserted. That night, on my return from New Haven, my nerves would seem slightly rattled, even while waiting for a taxi at Grand Central. All the same, many young people, though no longer the "flower children" of

« flower children » de naguère, n'ont pas cessé de rêver d'une rénovation de la société par une expérience morale. En réaction au puritanisme et à sa hantise du mal ils veulent penser que le mal n'est pas.

Pour New Haven j'ai pris un train au début de l'après-midi et je me retrouve bientôt, avec l'ami qui est venu m'accueillir, à l'orée du campus de Yale où je dois faire je ne sais plus aujourd'hui quelle causerie vers cinq heures. Et comme nous passons devant les églises voici que nous croisons un groupe de trois ou quatre personnes, dont Borges. Il est à Yale ce jour-là pour y parler lui aussi, le soir. Mais ce ne sera pas, me dit-il, une conférence, seulement une table ronde devant des étudiants qui lui poseront des questions. « Et d'ailleurs, me dit-il, puisque vous êtes ici, et libre, pourquoi ne viendriez-vous pas vous asseoir, vous aussi, à cette table ? » J'accepte l'invitation et chacun reprend son chemin. Nous savons que nous nous croiserons à nouveau au Faculty Club. Lui pour un repas avant cette table ronde, nous pour celui qui doit faire suite à mon exposé, et qu'on abrègera s'il le faut.

Les deux tables sont côte à côte et simultanément perçoivent de légers bruits, des frémissements, des rumeurs venant de la rue. Bientôt nous sortons, et comme dans un rêve nous voici dans une foule inaccoutumée, qui grossit à mesure que nous approchons de notre destination. Borges voyage avec son secrétaire, et celui-ci porte sa valise, mais cette cohue les sépare, nous perdons de vue nous aussi le vieil écrivain, nous nous inquiétons, tout de même nous nous retrouvons devant la salle où la table ronde doit se tenir.

Mais c'est pour apprendre que la règle de « full occupancy » interdit qu'elle ait lieu ici. Le public est évidemment déjà trop nombreux et on ne peut demander aux uns, dans ce désordre, de céder à

some time back, still dreamed of renovating society through a moral experiment. Reacting to Puritanism and its obsession with evil, they wanted to believe that evil doesn't exist.

I'd boarded my train to New Haven in the early afternoon; and soon I reached the edge of the campus, with a friend who'd picked me up at the station. At five o'clock, I was supposed to give a talk at Yale on something—I no longer remember what. As we were walking past the churches, we ran into a group of three or four people, Borges among them. He'd also come to the university to speak, later on that evening. But it wouldn't be a lecture, he told me, just a roundtable with an audience of students, there to ask him questions. "By the way," he went on, "since you're free at that hour, why don't you join our discussion, too?" I accepted the invitation, and each of us continued on his way. We knew we'd see each other again later on at the Faculty Club: he'd be dining there before the roundtable, and I'd be eating the meal that followed my talk—a repast we could cut short, if need be.

The two tables were side by side, and before long we heard a faint hubbub: stirs and rustlings that reached us from the street. After a while, we went outside. As in a dream, we were engulfed by an unaccustomed crowd; it ballooned larger and larger, the more we neared our destination. Borges was traveling with a secretary who carried his briefcase, and they were separated in the crush. We also lost sight of the elderly writer, and fretted over his whereabouts for several minutes. But in the end, we all converged in front of the hall where the roundtable would take place.

We were then advised that the "full occupancy" rule forbade us to hold it there: the public was already too numerous for a hall that could

d'autres leur droit d'entrer dans une salle où on ne peut être que deux ou trois cents, tout au plus. Il faut donc repartir vers une autre plus grande et on en a trouvé une. Mais la foule n'a pas cessé de grossir, aussi par curiosité pour ce qui se passe, si inusuel, et à la nouvelle porte c'est la même constatation. La capacité d'accueil est insuffisante et l'entrée sévèrement interdite. Il faut que tout ce flot vire sur soi et reflue.

Que faire ? Il y a bien quelque part un amphithéâtre à l'échelle, lui, du besoin, mais va-t-on pouvoir se le faire ouvrir ? Nous y allons et à quelques-uns, debout dans la cour derrière l'amphithéâtre, nous attendons, il fait nuit maintenant, et froid. Et je dis à Borges, entendant ces clameurs de toutes parts : « Voyez, vous êtes en train de déclencher la seconde révolution américaine ».

Borges n'était pas un révolutionnaire. Il tourna vers moi son beau visage où ne cessait jamais d'errer ce qui semblait de l'étonnement, et me dit : « Savez-vous ce à quoi je pense, en ce moment ? Je suis à Genève, au Bourg-du-Four ».

Le Bourg-du-Four, la place centrale du vieux Genève, le lieu par excellence où des existences réglées se croisent, aux différentes heures d'une journée qui répète celle d'avant. Ce n'est pas là que le jeune Argentin qui préparait son bachot dans la cité de Calvin à jamais prospère pouvait avoir été incité à des pensées révolutionnaires. Je lus pourtant, quelques années plus tard, ce récit, « L'autre », où Borges, à Cambridge encore, imagine qu'il rencontre sur un banc devant la rivière celui qu'il avait été dans ces années-là, et apprend de lui, en fait se souvient, que cet étudiant a commencé d'écrire des « Hymnes rouges », parce qu'il veut chanter « la fraternité de tous les hommes ». Et je crois donc qu'en ce soir de 1974 aussi c'est à cette époque de sa

only accommodate two or three hundred, at most. In the midst of this confusion, we couldn't expect people to forgo their right to attend; we had to head for a bigger venue, located in due course. But the throng kept growing steadily—somewhat out of curiosity, by now, since the event appeared to be exceptional. At the second hall, we were shunted away with the same announcement: insufficient capacity, no entry allowed. The whole tide had to swerve, and flow back again.

What next? There certainly was an amphitheater vast enough for our purpose, but would they unlock it for us? We stood around waiting for the people in charge, in the courtyard behind the building; by now night had fallen, and it was cold. Hearing the uproar on every side, I said to Borges: "It looks like you're inciting the second American Revolution."

Borges was not a revolutionary. He turned his beautiful face to me, on which a gleam of astonishment never ceased to roam. "Do you know what I'm thinking of, right now?" he asked me. "I'm in Geneva, at Bourg-du-Four."

Bourg-du-Four, the central square of old Geneva, is the quintessential setting where orderly lives coincide, at intervals, during a day which repeats the one before. It's not a place that could spark revolutionary urges in a teenage Argentine, working toward his high-school diploma in the prosperous city of Calvin. Even so, several years later I read a story by Borges called "The Other," which portrays him back in Cambridge again: there, on a bench beside the river, he comes across the young man he'd once been himself, long ago. He learns from the student—in fact, he remembers—that he's started writing a series of "Red Hymns," because he wants to sing "the brotherhood of all mankind." I suspect that on that evening in 1974, too, Borges was thinking

vie que Borges pensait. Il entendait dans la rue voisine s'enfler une espérance dont aujourd'hui c'était lui, bien bizarrement, qui en était l'occasion. Et il se demandait une fois de plus ce qu'il faut penser de ce qu'on croit à vingt ans. Est-ce, cette croyance, une des formes de l'éternelle illusion ? N'est-ce pas, à découvert un instant, la seule expérience qui puisse donner sens à la vie ?

Quelques minutes plus tard nous étions dans la salle qui était immense, en effet, et immensément pleine de jeunes gens survoltés. Le modérateur de la soirée énonça le nom des participants qui, chacun, de confiance, furent objet d'ovation, rien pourtant à côté des cris de joie qui saluèrent Borges, lequel indiqua, poliment, qu'il répondrait aux questions qu'on lui ferait passer sur de petits bouts de papier. Ce qui eut lieu. Questions et réponses se succédèrent, la salle bouillonna toute la soirée comme un banc de mer entre ses rochers, mais vint le moment où Borges eut à dire qu'il ne répondrait plus qu'à une question. Et lui fut remis le dernier mot griffonné.

Était-il si mal écrit, ou la vue de Borges était-elle vraiment réduite à à peu près rien ? Comme je l'avais vu faire à Cambridge il approcha la petite feuille de ses yeux, la fit glisser tout contre eux, et alors en déchiffra le seul mot, le seul point d'interrogation, et l'énonça à voix haute, avec ce suspens dans l'intonation de qui n'est encore qu'à préparer sa réponse.

« Love ? Yes », dit-il ainsi, s'apprêtant à enchaîner, mais la salle préféra prendre ce oui à son sens le plus fort, et absolu, et confiant, et d'un bond se mit debout pour une acclamation qui ce soir-là n'eut pas de fin, elle durait encore, tard dans la nuit, quand je repris la voie du retour pour retrouver New York en proie à son inquiétude. Jamais la loi de Friedlander, qui veut en histoire de l'art que l'on tue son père et

about this facet of his life. In the nearby street, he could hear the rising wind of a hope; but today it was he himself, strangely, who'd inspired it. And he wondered, all over again, what we're to make of the beliefs we cherish at age twenty. Are they merely figments of the eternal illusion? Aren't they, revealed for a moment, the only experience that gives meaning to our life?

A few minutes later, we sat down at the table: the hall was truly immense, and immensely packed with overexcited young people. The moderator introduced the participants by name, and each of us received a goodwill ovation. But this was nothing compared to the cries of joy that greeted Borges, who politely agreed to answer questions, if submitted to him on slips of paper. And so it went: questions and answers swung back and forth; all evening, the auditorium seethed like an ocean swell in a rocky cove. But the moment arrived when Borges had to say he'd reply to a final question, and the last scribbled note was handed up to the front.

Was it that badly scrawled, or was the author's vision really reduced to almost nil? As I'd seen him do in Cambridge, Borges held the strip of paper right against his eyes; he deciphered a single word, followed by a question mark. He pronounced it out loud, with the trailing tone that precedes a response.

"Love? Yes . . ." he said, gearing up to go on. But the hall preferred to take this yes in its strongest sense—as an affirmation of absolute trust. The crowd jumped up as one, to hurrah Borges with a wild acclaim that never seemed to end. It was still resounding, late into the night, when I set out for New York, gripped by its anxiety. Friedlander claims that in the history of art, we kill our father only to find our

redécouvre donc, avec émotion, son grand-père, ne fut si bien démontrée. Borges naissait de Nixon comme Phénix de ses cendres.

(Tout autre chose, cette soirée, que la cohue qui environna Borges au Collège de France sept ans plus tard. Là encore la foule avait peu à peu grossi, à la fin on entrait dans la salle 8 par défoncement des fenêtres mais c'était curiosité bien plus que ferveur, et même quelque hostilité était perceptible parmi ces gens qui se côtoyaient sans se savoir. J'interprétai ainsi, en tout cas, la question, jetée à voix haute et de loin à travers la salle : « Monsieur Borges, vous qui êtes aveugle, que pensez-vous du cinéma ? »)

III

Troisième souvenir, la dernière rencontre, à Genève, à l'hôpital cantonal où Borges, venu achever sa vie près du Bourg-du-Four, est soigné pour quelques semaines. C'est bien peu de temps avant sa mort.

Je suis venu lui faire visite avec Jean Starobinski. Dans la petite chambre nous sommes assis de part et d'autre du lit. Borges est affaibli mais toujours aussi bienveillant, aussi gracieux. Et, je ne sais plus pourquoi ni comment, j'en suis venu à parler de Virgile, lequel n'est pas sans avoir beaucoup compté pour Borges.

« Virgile ? dit Borges. Oui, mais n'oubliez pas Verlaine ! » Et de Verlaine il parla une fois de plus dans sa vie, puis il fut question d'autre chose et enfin nous prîmes congé. Borges se souleva alors sur son coude. « N'oubliez pas Verlaine », me dit-il. Puis, comme nous franchissions la porte, d'une voix plus forte il dit à nouveau : « Virgile *et* Verlaine », en accentuant ce « et » qui signifiait une équivalence mais

grandfather again, who moves us to deep emotion. Never had his rule of thumb been proven so well: Borges emerged from Nixon like the phoenix from his ashes.

(That evening at Yale was very different from the tumult over Borges at the Collège de France, seven years later. There again, the crowd had expanded bit by bit, until at last people were climbing into Auditorium 8 by breaking the windows. But this time, the curiosity far outstripped the fervor, and I even whiffed some hostility in the disparate, unknowing multitude. In any case, that's how I interpreted a question shouted from the back of the hall: "Monsieur Borges, since you're blind, what do you think of the cinema?")

III

A third recollection: our last meeting, at the cantonal hospital in Geneva. Borges, who'd elected to round out his life near the Bourg-du-Four, was treated there for several weeks.

Shortly before his death, I visited him with Jean Starobinski. In the small room, we were seated on either side of his bed. Though weakened, Borges was as gracious and benevolent as ever. I can't recall why or how, but I brought up the subject of Virgil, who'd always signified so much to him.

"Virgil?" said Borges. "Yes, but don't forget Verlaine!" And he spoke about Verlaine, once more in this life; after that, we passed on to something else, and finally took our leave. Borges propped himself up on his elbow. "Don't forget Verlaine," he told me. Then, as we were walking through the door, he raised his voice: "Virgil *and* Verlaine." By emphasizing the "and," he'd pointed to an equivalence; but above

surtout une complémentarité qu'il estimait nécessaire à la pensée de la poésie.

Et nous étions déjà à quelques pas de la chambre dans le couloir quand je l'entendis répéter, à voix encore plus forte, un troisième « Virgile *et* Verlaine ». Ce rappel, ce message de tant de sens dans si peu de mots, ce sont les dernières paroles que j'aurai entendues de lui.

all, he aimed to stress a complementarity, crucial to our meditation of poetry.

When we were already in the hallway, a few steps down from the room, Borges repeated in an even louder voice: "Virgil *and* Verlaine." These words—a message with so much meaning, so briefly expressed—were the last I heard him say.

FROM LA LONGUE CHAÎNE DE L'ANCRE

THE ANCHOR'S LONG CHAIN

ALES STENAR

I

On dit
Que des barques paraissent dans le ciel,
Et que, de quelques-unes,
La longue chaîne de l'ancre peut descendre
Vers notre terre furtive.
L'ancre cherche sur nos prairies, parmi nos arbres,
Le lieu où s'arrimer,
Mais bientôt un désir de là-haut l'arrache,
Le navire d'ailleurs ne veut pas d'ici,
Il a son horizon dans un autre rêve.

Il advient, toutefois,
Que l'ancre soit, dirait-on, lourde, inusuellement,
Et traîne presque au sol et froisse les arbres.
On l'aurait vue se prendre à une porte d'église,
Sous le cintre où s'efface notre espoir,
Et quelqu'un de cet autre monde fût descendu,
Gauchement, le long de la chaîne tendue, violente,
Pour délivrer son ciel de notre nuit.
Ah, quelle angoisse, quand il travailla contre la voûte,
Prenant à pleines mains son étrange fer,
Pourquoi faut-il
Que quelque chose en nous leurre l'esprit
Dans cette traversée que la parole
Tente, sans rien savoir, vers son autre rive ?

ALES STENAR

I

They say
Boats appear in the sky;
And from some of them,
The anchor's long chain trails down
To our hidden, fleeting earth.
On our prairies, among our trees, the anchor hunts
A place to moor—but soon, a higher will
Wrenches it loose.
Elsewhere's ship does not want a here:
Its horizon opens in some other dream.

Even so, it can happen:
Maybe the anchor, heavier than usual,
Drags near the ground, rumpling the trees.
We almost see it catch on a church door,
Under the arch where our hope fades away.
Awkwardly, someone from that other world
Clambers down the taut, lurching chain,
To deliver his sky from our night.
What anguish, as he works against the vault,
Grappling with his strange iron hook . . .
Why must something within us
Lure the mind, in this crossing
Our words attempt, unknowingly,
To reach their other shore?

II

Le prince de ce pays, que voulait-il
Quand il fit rassembler, sur la falaise,
Tant de pierres debout, pour imiter
La forme d'un navire, qui partirait
Un jour, sur cette mer entre ciel et monde,
Et, toujours hésitant, presque désemparé,
Peut-être rejoindrait enfin le port
Que d'aucuns cherchent dans la mort, imaginée
Vie plus intense, une ligne de feux
À l'horizon désert d'une longue côte ?
La nef de son désir,
Cette proue dans le roc, ces beaux flancs courbes,
Va immobile. Et moi je cherche à lire
Dans l'immobilité le mouvement
Qu'il imprima au rêve, lui qui savait
Qu'il mourrait au combat, contre des hommes
Masqués et s'exclamant dans une autre langue
De ce monde d'ici où rien, jamais,
Ne dure que l'étonnement et la douleur.

Un inconnu parmi eux lui fait signe,
Un envoyé de là-bas sur la mer,
Il est tout de lumière blanche, dans la fumée,
Et lui, il rend les coups, il ahane, il crie,
Mais déjà, avec l'ange qui lui sourit,
Il se tait, il s'est établi dans cette cabine

II

What did he want, the prince of this land,
When he had so many tall stones
Raised upright on a cliff, to rhyme
The form of a ship? Maybe to depart
One day, on this sea between world and sky—
Though still faltering, almost in distress—
And at last, perhaps to enter that port
Some would seek in death, imagined
As a life more intense, a glimmer of lights
On the sweep of an empty coast.
The vessel, the nave of his desire,
This prow in rock, this beautiful curved hull,
Moves motionless. I try to read
In immobility the going forth
He printed on his dream, as one who knew
He'd die in combat with visored men—
Masks who'd shout in another tongue
From the world of here, where nothing
Ever lasts, but bewilderment and pain.

Among them, a stranger beckons to him now—
An envoy from out there, on the sea—his whiteness
Wholly luminous amid the smoke.
The prince strikes blow for blow, he grunts and yells;
But falling silent at the angel's smile,
He takes his place forward on the ship.

À l'avant du navire, ils sont assis
Maintenant l'un auprès de l'autre, à une table
Où rien n'est plus des cartes, des portulans
De cette vie d'ici, ni des nourritures,
Ni même des images, que sa mémoire
Lui offrait, de ses mains faciles, la nuit venue
Dans l'étrange pays où l'on naît et meurt.
Mémoire d'autres heures que les combats,
Mémoire de paroles réprimées,
Mémoire de la douceur qui est obscure
Comme le vin qui alourdit la grappe,
Mémoire de l'aperçu mais incompris
Et de moments trop brefs d'affections gauches.

Il rêva, il partit. Mais aujourd'hui, ici,
Ce n'est rien devant nous et autour de nous
Que le ciel de ce monde, rayons, nuées,
Puis, sur les pierres qui noircissent et se confondent,
La flèche du tonnerre et soudain la pluie.
Toute une eau véhémente nous enveloppe,
Les stèles ne sont plus qu'une seule présence
Là ou là surgissante, disparaissante,
Bien qu'entre elles coure l'éclair. Et je veux croire
Que cette flamme, c'est une paix, et qu'elle embrasse,
Avec infiniment d'émotion, de joie,
Un qui lutte dans ce désordre, à gauche, à droite,
Contre trop d'assaillants, et va mourir.

There in the cabin, side by side, they sit
Together: at a table cleared of the meals,
The nautical charts, the playing cards of a life
Lived here. Even the pictures are gone:
His memory had dealt them with an easygoing hand,
When night would overtake
Our odd country of birth and death.
Memory of hours without war,
Memory of words held back,
Memory of sweetness dark
As wine clustered in grapes,
Memory of inklings misjudged,
And moments of clumsy affection,
All too brief.

He dreamed; he set sail. But here, today,
Before us and around us, there's nothing
But the sky of this world—clouds, rays of light;
Then, on the stones that blacken and merge,
The thunder's arrow; and suddenly, the rain.
Headlong, a downpour engulfs us, and now
The steles shape a single presence, bursting
Into view, there and there again—until it vanishes,
Though the lightning still runs through them.
I want to believe
This flame is peace, bestowed with infinite joy
On the fighter who's outnumbered in the mayhem,
Left and right, and who will die.

Plus tard, me retournant
Vers le navire de pierre, sous le ciel
Redevenu celui des matins d'été
(Et que faire, sinon se retourner
Dans cette vie où rien n'est qui ne passe ?),
Je vois que sur la pierre voulue la proue
Un grand oiseau de mer s'est posé : un instant
De l'immobilité mystérieuse dont est
Capable une vie simple, sans langage.
L'oiseau regarde au loin, écoute, espère,
Il mène le navire, et d'autres, d'autres,
Sont là, autour de lui, au-dessus de lui,
À crier et à s'effacer dans le sillage.

Later, turning back
To the ship of rock, under skies
Of summer morning once again
(And what can we do but turn back,
In this life where nothing stands still?),
I see a big seabird alight
On the stone meant for a prow: an instant
Of the mystery, motionless and wordless,
A simple life can live. The bird looks off
Into the distance; he listens, and hopes.
He guides the ship on—and others, others
Surround him with their cries; around him,
Above him, they fade into the wake.

L'AMÉRIQUE

En ce temps-là j'habitais une petite maison isolée parmi quelques autres sur une colline de sable et d'herbe courte et très claire. J'en sortais tôt le matin et me dirigeais vers un restaurant que j'apercevais à un ou deux kilomètres, juste de l'autre côté de la route qui suit à quelque distance la côte du Pacifique. C'était pour moi un plaisir, voir ces voitures là-bas se croiser en silence sur tout ce ruban de route au rebord de la campagne déserte, voir aussi les fenêtres du restaurant dont les feux de la nuit étaient allumés encore, malgré la belle lumière dorée des aubes de ce pays. Devant ces vitrages passaient des ombres, celle d'une automobile qui s'arrêtait, d'une ou deux personnes qui s'approchaient d'une porte. Je descendais par un chemin sans rigueur vers cette vie qui semblait encore d'un autre monde, bien que le bruit m'en fût devenu à un moment perceptible, puis se fût accru par degrés; et les événements de ces minutes paisibles, ce n'était jamais que l'étoile brusque d'un pare-chocs se heurtant à un rayon de soleil ou, sur la longue et basse montagne bleue que je laissais à ma droite, l'enflammement passager d'un champ de moutarde. En bref, la vie quotidienne de la lumière, quelque chose comme une intimité surprise mais qui d'emblée voulait bien, et rassurait. La lumière était mon amie, elle resterait avec moi tout ce jour encore.

Mais ce jour-là, un dimanche, quel changement après tous ces matins qui avaient été les mêmes, une façon pour le temps de couler sans bruit, comme ces courants que l'eau a parfois au milieu des plages quand la marée se retire ! La route que je pouvais, de la distance où j'étais, suivre des yeux sur des kilomètres était tout à fait sans voitures. Et à la place de ce flux régulier des autres jours je distinguais

AMERICA

Back then I lived in a small house among several others, on an isolated sand hill, sown with short, bright-green grass. I set out early every morning, and headed for a restaurant visible a mile or so away, just across the road that hugs the Pacific coast. I loved to watch the cars as they streamed by silently below, skirting the open countryside, on that long ribbon of road. I enjoyed watching the windows of the restaurant, too, still lit up for night despite the golden dawn, always so lovely in that region. Shadows crossed the sheets of glass—cast by a car pulling up, or one or two people approaching a door. I strolled down the path on an easy slope, toward that life from another world; though at some point, its sounds became audible, gradually louder. The events of those peaceful minutes were little more than a bumper's sudden star, as it nicked a sunbeam; or the transient flare of a mustard field, on the low blue mountain to my right. In short, I shared the everyday existence of the light: a bit as though I'd intruded on its privacy, but found right away it reassured me, and wished me well. The light was my friend, and would stay with me the whole day through.

But then, after all those mornings that had always been the same—a way for time to flow by noiselessly, like rivulets left on the beach by an ebbing tide—what a change took place one day, a Sunday. From my distant perch, the view was clear for miles; but now I couldn't see a single car. Instead of the usual traffic, today I made out what seemed to

des groupes de ce qui semblait bien être des enfants, groupes sans nombre qui allaient tous dans le même sens et, surgissant de sous l'horizon du nord pour se perdre à celui du sud, paraissaient d'autant moins relever de la réalité ordinaire qu'ils occupaient fantastiquement toute la durée de leur passage sur terre à faire avancer à divers niveaux dans le ciel de grands ballons de couleurs nombreuses, souvent brillantes, et de formes encore plus étonnantes. Certaines de celles-ci très pures, les cinq corps simples, une parfaite beauté de plans et d'arêtes au service d'une matière, étoffe sans doute, translucide; et d'autres complexes, enchevêtrées, même parfois vaguement bouffonnes avec alors des prolongements sans raison visible, bras et jambes nantis de bracelets ou de souliers de lumière. Les enfants retenaient ces ballons par des fils qui leur assuraient un semblant de liberté, vécue avec bonne humeur. Et si quelques-uns de ces frêles aérostats suivaient simplement, à la verticale, le petit être, là-bas, qui en avait le contrôle, d'autres titubaient, trébuchaient en riant, dragons gauches et débonnaires, et d'autres enfin semblaient errer d'un point à un autre du cortège sinon même des deux côtés de la route. Brillaient les fils de soie, s'opacifiaient ici ou là le rouge grenat, le bleu violacé ou le jaune d'une de ces toiles gonflées comme des voiles, s'entrechoquaient quelques-unes d'elles.

Et au sol, à des moments, quelques pas de chaussée sans rien ni personne, mais le cortège — où il y avait des enfants pour s'arrêter, rebrousser chemin, passer d'un groupe à un autre — se reformait vite aussi serré que précédemment, et je découvrais même, de plus en plus étonné à mesure que je m'approchais de la route, que c'était vraiment une grande foule, et qu'il y avait ici et là dans ses rangs une

be children: countless groups of children, all walking in the same direction, spilling over the horizon from the north, and dipping out of sight to the south. They appeared to spring from no humdrum reality: all the more, since they spent their whole passage on earth amid a fantasy, moving huge balloons across the sky, staggered at different heights. Their colors were wildly varied, often bright, and their shapes were even more astonishing. Some were pure: the five solid bodies of geometry; a perfect beauty of planes and angles, formed from a lucid material—some kind of cloth, no doubt. Others were tangled and complex—even, at times, vaguely clownish. They sprouted growths that defied any purpose: arms adorned with bracelets, or legs wearing shoes of light. The children held on to these balloons with strings that allowed them a semblance of freedom, savored with bonhomie. While some of the frail aerostats merely coasted ahead, straight above their puny guides, others reeled and tottered with laughter, like clumsy, good-natured dragons. Still others seemed to wander here and there in the parade, or even to veer widely, on either side of the road. The silken strings glistened, and now and then, a purplish blue, pomegranate red, or yellow turned opaque. The curving sheets bulged like sails, and some of the balloons jostled in midair.

On the ground, intermittently, a gap appeared—several feet of pavement, empty of anyone or anything. Children stopped, retraced their steps, or joined a different group; but the procession soon filled in again, as densely as before. More and more astounded, the nearer I drew to the road, I now discerned the crowd was truly enormous. Its

variété de menues énigmes comme je n'en aurais pas soupçonnées l'instant d'avant. Parfois ce n'était pas des piétons, ce qui avançait, mais des cyclistes, tenant d'une main le fil du ballon, qui pouvait pourtant être plutôt vaste, une sorte de montgolfière, crachant du feu; parfois c'étaient, poussés, traînés par les garçons et les filles, des chariots découverts où se dressait, oscillant, tanguant, ce qui du coup semblait des statues avec elles aussi des flammes sur leurs épaules, ou tout au moins beaucoup de fumée, une vapeur rousse dont maintenant je sentais même l'odeur, où il y avait de l'encens. La file était sans fin, et sans nombre tout aussi bien les occasions de surprise. L'impression d'étrangeté absolue qui se dégageait de ce grand cortège encore pour moi presque silencieux n'était pas plus forte que celle de l'infini que je me plaisais à y ressentir. Les sauterelles qui s'abattent sur les jardins d'une ville, la dernière avant le désert, ne sont pas, j'imagine, plus mystérieuses, petites vies aux yeux clos sous leurs tiares de souverains sans royaume. Mais plus encore que de l'étonnement, ce qui s'emparait de moi, c'était cette allégresse qui naît de ce qui surprend sans qu'on ait moyen de comprendre: cette joie qu'on a d'espérer que vont se rompre les chaînes de l'entendement d'hier, de toujours, et qu'à ne plus savoir on va enfin être davantage.

II

Partagé ainsi, en tout cas, entre l'émerveillement et la réflexion, j'étais arrivé à la route, je passais de l'herbe à l'asphalte et commençais — hier encore les voitures se fussent arrêtées, sereinement, pour me laisser traverser — à me frayer un passage vers le petit déjeuner à travers ces groupes qui ne me prêtaient aucune attention, tout oc-

ranks held a range of small enigmas I hadn't suspected before. Some were not pedestrians, but cyclists, tugging their string with only one hand; even so, the aerostat they trailed might be fairly immense—a kind of hot-air balloon, spitting fire. Other boys and girls were pushing or pulling open carts, where statues nodded and swayed. The shoulders of these effigies also gave off flames, or smoke at least—russet fumes, thick with an incense I could already smell. The line was endless, and so were the occasions for surprise. Still beyond my hearing, this grand cortege impressed me by its absolute strangeness; but my delight at the infinity I sensed in it was just as deep. Locusts sweeping down on the gardens of a city, the last before the desert, are no less mysterious, I imagine: tiny lives, eyes shut beneath their tiaras, like monarchs without a kingdom. Even more than amazement, what seized me was gladness, the joy that's born when something overtakes us we have no way to grasp: the hope of breaking the chains of insights that always bound us until now—the joyous hope that by no longer knowing, we will at last more fully be.

II

At any rate, half in wonder, half in thought, I'd reached the road by now. I stepped from the grass onto the asphalt—yesterday, the cars would've stopped serenely, to let me cross—and elbowed my way to breakfast. Busy as they were with the yells, laughs, calls, and hur-

cupés qu'ils étaient par des cris, des rires, des exclamations, des appels lancés d'un de ces essaims vers un autre. Et j'entrai dans le restaurant où, telles des sauterelles chues du nuage, plusieurs de ces enfants ou jeunes adolescents en blue-jeans classiquement délavés, T-shirts ou Bermuda shorts, étaient eux-mêmes entrés pour boire des breuvages rouges ou blancs, certains jaunes. Ils étaient donc tout près de moi désormais, certains même étaient seuls devant leur orangeade ou sirop d'orgeat, j'aurais pu essayer de m'enquérir auprès de l'un de ceux-ci des raisons de cet exode vers le désert, mais je me gardai de le faire. Il me suffisait de penser qu'il n'y avait aucun sinistre joueur de flûte à l'avant de leur premier groupe, parmi les dunes.

Je ne questionnais pas, je ne cherchais pas à savoir: mais c'est aussi parce que quelqu'un en moi me disait que c'était bien inutile, que ce n'aurait pu être que l'occasion de propos pour rien, de petites erreurs à constater avec amusement et oublier tout de suite, parce qu'en fait je savais déjà, mieux que ces enfants qui riaient, qui bienheureusement ne pensaient qu'à se bousculer et à rire, ce qui était en jeu dans le grand cortège. Un très gros ballon, certainement plus volumineux, de beaucoup même, que tous les autres, venait de passer, avec sursauts et reflets, devant les vitres du restaurant, il en restait une lueur rouge, il était donc facile d'imaginer qu'il allait être lancé, là-bas au sud, bien au delà des mille essors plus minimes, vers un point de chute qui ne pourrait être que loin sur le continent ou en mer, le hasard allait donc être le dieu de cette journée: voila déjà qui me laissait pressentir ce que signifiait ce rassemblement, cette fête. Et je commençais à comprendre bien d'autres choses que celle-ci, je voyais s'éclairer le sens de cette civilisation, l'Amérique, qui depuis tant d'années m'était de-

rahs they bandied back and forth from group to group, the swarming throng paid me no mind. When I entered the restaurant, I saw several of these youngsters, already in their teens: they, too, had landed there, like locusts fallen from the cloud. Dressed in T-shirts, and classic faded jeans or Bermuda shorts, they sipped on red, white, or yellow beverages. From then on, I had them at close range. A few even sat all alone, before an orange soda or lemon-and-lime. It would've been easy to sound them out about this exodus into the desert; but instead, I held my tongue. For me, it was enough to assume no dire piper headed up their column, marching them through the dunes.

I didn't question them; I didn't try to find out. Partly because someone inside me argued it was useless: it would only lead to jejune remarks, petty mistakes corrected with amusement, and forgotten right away. In fact, I already knew better than these fun-loving children—who blissfully thought about nothing, but laughing and horsing around—what was really at stake, in this vast parade. A tremendous balloon, larger by far than all the others, had just careened past the restaurant windows, lurching and shimmering. Its reddish glow lingered still. I could readily imagine it being launched—down there to the south, far beyond the thousand lesser flights—toward a distant point of fall, over the continent or the sea: so chance would be the god of this day. That already gave me an inkling of what the festive gathering must signify. And I began to understand many other things, too. The meaning of America dawned on me, clear as day. It was a civiliza-

venue si proche mais non sans me rester un peu étrangère, en fait je déchiffrais toutes les énigmes, j'en venais même à élucider quelques événements de ma propre vie sur lesquels j'avais de toujours buté avec étonnement et tristesse. C'était comme si ce qui s'était présenté à mes yeux sur cette route en Californie n'était pas seulement un événement mais un signe, dont l'effet serait désormais de déployer ma pensée à l'image de ces polyèdres aux faces légèrement colorées que je voyais passer quelquefois encore: facettes de l'être même. — Toute une intuition, tout un étagement d'idées que je me mis à noter, sur un coin de table d'abord, puis en m'arrêtant à des talus ou de grosses pierres sur le chemin du retour vers la petite maison sur la colline.

Et ces notations, ce n'était sur la feuille froissée au creux de la main que de brèves phrases, très elliptiques, parfois deux mots. Mais peu importe ! J'aurais bien le temps tout à l'heure — et demain, et dans les années à venir — de donner forme plus explicite et complète à l'explication de l'Amérique, et de tout, que j'avais prise vivante dans mon filet.

III

L'après-midi, toutefois, je pensais à autre chose; puis je revins à Paris, je laissai les semaines, les mois, les années s'écouler sans que je reprisse mes notes, jusqu'au jour où je me dis que le moment était venu tout de même de rédiger « L'Amérique ». Sur quoi je recherchai les deux ou trois feuillets jaunes, arrachés d'un bloc de là-bas, où entre les lignes qui y étaient légèrement imprimées s'effaçait déjà le crayon, à cause des séjours qu'avait faits ce papier plié, replié, dans les manteaux du voyage puis le désordre des tables. Je défroissai mes notes, je

tion I'd grown close to over the years, though it remained a bit foreign. But now I'd deciphered all its mysteries. I even managed to decode certain events in my own life that had always tripped me up, leaving me sad and bewildered. What had passed before my eyes, on that California road, seemed like more than just a happenstance: it was a sign. From this morning forward, my thoughts would unfold like those many-planed shapes I could still catch sight of, on and off, their sides lightly hued: they were facets of being, itself. My intuitions deepened, and ideas started mounting up. At first I noted them down at the edge of a table, and then as I paused at boulders, or embankments, on my way back up the hill to the little house.

My jottings were only brief phrases, highly elliptical: often just a word or two, scrawled on crumpled paper I held against my palm. But what difference did it make? I'd have plenty of time, later that day—and tomorrow, and in years to come—to mold and perfect the explanation of America, and of everything, that wriggled in my net.

III

But as it happened, that afternoon I had to turn to something else. I traveled back to Paris, and let weeks, months, years slip by, without revisiting my notes. Finally, I thought it was high time to compose "America"; and so I retrieved those two or three yellow sheets, torn from a notepad I'd used while I was there. They'd been folded up repeatedly, in the coats I'd worn on my trip, or the disorder of my desks—and so the pencil marks, between the faintly printed lines, had already faded. I smoothed out my notes and reread them—or tried to

les relus, ou plutôt j'essayai de les relire car, au premier regard puis au second et après encore — un questionnement de plus en plus perplexe, et quelque contrariété —, je n'y découvris aucun sens. Des mots, mais dont la pensée s'était retirée. Là où aurait dû reparaître la cohérence plus forte qu'ils avaient perçue et notée, rien même qui s'ébauchât, j'en venais à prendre quelques-unes des marques du crayon gris sur le papier chiffonné pour de simples traits, sans raison tracés en deçà — plutôt qu'au delà — du langage.

Et je me posai des questions. N'avais-je pas su noter les idées que j'avais eues en cette matinée de Californie, avais-je alors trop imprudemment fait confiance à ma mémoire, et une pensée qui avait du sens et aurait maintenant du prix s'était-elle ainsi bien réellement évaporée du griffonnement de ces pages, me laissant privé, à jamais peut-être, de ma vérité la plus essentielle ? Ou avais-je rêvé, au moment même où j'écrivais ou croyais écrire ? Ce grand cortège, aussi fantastique me parût-il, avait bien eu lieu dans ce qu'on appelle la réalité éveillée, je le voyais bien trop clairement — je le vois maintenant encore —, mais au delà? Au delà dans l'esprit qui interprète les signes? Au delà dans les souvenirs, les fantasmes — et les illuminations mais tôt après les censures — que réveillent avec violence les événements imprévus ? Mes trois pages de notes ne ressemblaient à rien tant qu'à ces mots sans haut ni bas, sans forme ni contenu, qu'en se réveillant le matin on découvre avec déception sur la feuille où pendant la nuit on les a notés, au débouché d'un grand rêve.

Je me posai ces questions, quelqu'un en moi voulait réfléchir, comprendre sinon l'Amérique et l'être du monde, du moins le jeu avec soi de ma pensée, de ma vie. Mais ce ne fut qu'un moment, cette

reread them. From the first glance, as I stared again and again, I grew steadily more baffled, not to say vexed. I couldn't make sense of my words anymore; whatever their meaning, it had wholly drained away. The coherence they'd spied and captured ought to be resurfacing, but even its outline had vanished. I had to dismiss a number of these gray squiggles, on rumpled paper, as little more than doodles: far from transcending language, they fell short of it.

I cross-examined myself. Had I really been so careless in scribbling down my ideas, that morning in California? Had I relied too rashly on my memory? Had thoughts that meant something then, and would've taken on new value for me now, simply leached from those scrawled-out notes—leaving me bereft, maybe forever, of my most essential truth? Or at the moment when I was writing—or thought I was writing—had I been dreaming instead? That grand cortege, fantastic though it seemed to me, had indeed taken place in what we call our waking reality. I saw it all too clearly—I still see it now. But beyond? In the inner mind, that interprets signs? In the memories, the hauntings, the revelations—with second guesses nipping at their heels—that unforeseen events arouse in us so fiercely? My three sheets of notes were like those words we dash down at night, at the end of a momentous dream. The next day, when we find them on the page, they disappoint us: we can't make head or tail of their content, or their form.

I mulled over these questions, since someone inside me still longed to get to the bottom of this. If America—much less the fundamental nature of the world—were too tall an order, at least I wanted to understand the game my thought, and my life, were playing with them-

perplexité, ce désir: car vite le papier que je regardais commença à s'assombrir, les mots qui m'y refusaient leur sens se mirent à bouger, à rougeoyer faiblement, et ce furent à nouveau des images, d'abord floues mais bientôt assez précises, comme si déjà je savais beaucoup de ce qui m'appelait à travers elles.

Que fut ce rêve? Eh bien, d'un cortège encore, mais celui-là sur un étroit sentier de montagne. Et d'écoliers cette fois encore, et de leurs ballons, mais dans une nuit épaisse et sous de grands vents. Les enfants — oui, tout à fait des enfants, on est encore plus jeune ici que sur l'autre route —, c'est sans hésiter pourtant qu'ils grimpent ces pentes on ne peut plus escarpées, où à des moments le passage est si étroit, entre deux rochers dont l'un surplombe le gouffre, qu'il faut qu'ils se bousculent pour ne pas rester sans fin sur ce seuil, si vertigineux! de plus avant dans la nuit. Ils vont, les yeux baissés. Au-dessus d'eux la masse presque invisible de ces ballons dont eux aussi retiennent le fil qui parfois casse, sous la poussée du vent, aveugle là-haut, étrangère au monde. Et moi, tantôt je suis repoussé au bord du sentier par leur avancée innombrable, tantôt je puis aller parmi eux, partageant alors les trébuchements de leur fatigue, percevant leur essoufflement, entendant ici ou là dans leur foule des rires brefs, de brusques débuts de chants qui s'interrompent tout aussi vite, et aussi des cris de souffrance, aussi des pleurs. Bruits dans l'espace de ces ballons qui se cognent, qui craquent, qui se déchirent, qui rebondissent sur les ondes d'air noir du ciel. Furtives traînées de feu à leurs flancs où brille alors, un instant, un peu de rouge ou de jaune. Et parfois le fracas d'un éboulement plus haut, bien plus haut, dans la montagne, mais tout cela, tout cela toujours, du silence. Le plus vaste des ballons vient de

selves. But my puzzlement, and my desire, lasted no more than an instant. Swiftly, the sheet of paper before my eyes began to darken. The words that denied me their meaning started to stir, to gleam with a feeble light. And now there were images again, blurred at first but soon fairly sharp, as though I'd foreknown why they summoned me.

What was the dream about? Well, a procession again, this one on a narrow mountain path. Schoolchildren gather once more, holding balloons, but now in the thick of night, under gusting winds. The children are very much children, younger here than on the other road; even so, they don't hesitate to clamber up these sheer rock slopes, unbelievably steep. In spots the passage threads along a crag, overhanging the abyss: it's so confined they have to scramble to squeeze by. No one wants to tarry on this dizzying brink, far into the night. They press forward, with downcast eyes. The clustering balloons, almost invisible overhead, strain against their hands. Now and then, a string snaps abruptly in the wind that rages blindly up there, alien to the world. At times, the countless hikers crowd me to the edge of the path; at others, I manage to walk with them, sharing their shortness of breath, their stumbling fatigue. Here and there, in the throng, I hear stabs at laughter; songs broken off, as soon as they start; and cries of suffering, children who weep aloud. The balloons ram each other noisily, split and rip, bounce on the waves of black air that surge through the sky. Trails of fire sneak along their flanks, flashing a glint of yellow or red. Sometimes a landslide crashes higher up—much higher up, on the mountain; but always, all around, there is silence. The most gigantic balloon of all lumbers over me, only the lowest part

passer au-dessus de moi, visible seulement par sa partie la plus basse, un filet que des flammes enveloppent sans qu'elles l'aient embrasé encore. Plus tard je l'apercevrai à nouveau, il semble s'être arrêté au-dessus d'une terre qu'on ne voit pas, que l'on n'atteindra jamais peut-être, dans les cailloux, sous cette fois tout le ciel, toutes les étoiles. Et voici qu'un enfant essaie de revenir en arrière, malgré l'étroitesse de la voie, — vers qui ? Il se heurte aux autres, eux si requis par la difficulté d'aller de l'avant et de retenir leurs ballons qu'ils ne le voient même pas. Je le prends par un bras, je le retiens. « Où vas-tu? », lui dis-je. Il lève vers moi deux yeux agrandis par une pensée dont jamais je ne saurai rien.

Et je lui ai demandé encore: « Comment t'appelles-tu ? » Mais sans répondre, et me regardant toujours, de ses yeux pensifs, il secoue la tête.

Je ne t'oublie jamais, enfant qui veut revenir, où, tu ne sais. Je t'aperçois à travers le moindre de tous ces mots que j'écris, même quand mes phases qui rêvent tiennent au bout de leurs fils tendus par un vent léger des sphères qui sont brillantes si ce n'est pas même très claires: que je pourrais croire brillantes de rosée, comme si le jour avait reparu sur terre. Je te sais au secret de tous les tableaux que j'aime. Je t'entends qui trébuche au fond pierreux des quelques livres que je lis, que je sache lire, visage fiévreux que je voudrais prendre dans mes mains. Et parfois je touche presque à ton front, à ton regard qui demande, mais alors ce sont tous ces signes qui se dissipent. Et avec eux le jour et la nuit, et même le monde, même le vent.

of it visible; though flames envelop its webbing, it hasn't caught fire, not yet. Later it looms into view once again: it seems to hover above a land we can't see, that we'll never reach, perhaps, among the stones—under the whole sky this time, and all the stars.

And here comes a child, trying to turn back, despite the trail's narrowness—who's he looking for? He bumps into the others; but they're struggling so hard to forge ahead, and keep a grip on their balloons, they don't even notice him. I seize him by the arm, I hold him back. "Where are you going?" I say. He looks up at me, his eyes enlarged by a thought I'll never know.

I ask him: "What's your name?" But with no reply, still staring with his pensive eyes, he shakes his head.

I never forget you, child who wants to go back—where, you can't tell. I glimpse you in every word I write, even when my sentences dream bright spheres at the end of their strings, tautened by gentle winds: spheres so luminous they seem to shine with dew, as though day had returned to the earth. I sense you in the secret of all the paintings I love. I hear you stumbling at the stony core of the only books I read, the few I know how to read. I long to hold your fevered face in my hands. At times, I almost touch your forehead, meet your questioning gaze—but then all these signs melt away. And with them the day and the night, and even the world, even the wind.

LE PEINTRE DONT LE NOM EST LA NEIGE

I

Quelle pourpre là-bas, du côté effondré du ciel !

La neige est donc venue cette nuit avec dans ses mains la couleur.

Tout ce qu'elle répand se nomme silence.

Adam et Ève passent sur le chemin, chaudement vêtus. Leurs pas ne font aucun bruit dans la neige qui couvre l'herbe.

Et la brume écarte pour eux de légers rideaux, c'est une salle parmi les arbres, puis c'en est une autre et une autre encore.

Un écureuil s'ébroue, de trop de lumière.

Personne n'est jamais venu dans ces bois, pas même celui qui donne nom et s'angoisse d'avoir donné nom et en meurt,

Dieu qui n'est plus que la neige.

II

Ce peintre qui est penché sur sa toile, je le touche à l'épaule, il sursaute, il se retourne, c'est la neige.

THE PAINTER NAMED SNOW

I

What a purple over there, on the crumbled side of the sky . . .

Snow must've come tonight, with color in his hands.

Silence is the name of all he sows.

Warmly dressed, Adam and Eve walk by on the path. Snow covers the grass, so their steps don't crunch.

For them, the mist draws back its flimsy curtains: there's a room between the trees, then another, then another.

A squirrel shakes himself, from too much light.

No one has ever come to these woods, even the giver of names. His grief over giving names has killed him off:

God who's nothing now but snow.

II

A painter bends over his canvas . . . I tap him on the shoulder. He gives a start and turns around: he's the snow.

Son visage est sans fin, ses mains sans nombre, il se lève, il passe à gauche et à droite de moi, et au-dessus de moi par milliers de flocons qui se font de plus en plus serrés, de plus en plus clairs. Je regarde derrière moi, c'est partout la neige.

Son pinceau : une fumée de la cime des arbres, qui se dissipent, qui le dissipent.

III

Et à des moments je ne vois plus rien que ma chaussure qui troue la blancheur crissante. Le bleu vif des lacets, l'ocre de la toile de grain serré, les marques brunes qu'y laisse la neige qui s'en détache dès que mon pas s'en dégage pour me porter en avant, dans des remous de lumière.

Le peintre qui se nomme la neige a bien travaillé, ce matin encore. Il a rajeuni le dessin des branches, le ciel est un enfant qui court en riant vers moi, je resserre autour de son cou la grosse écharpe de laine.

His face is endless, his hands are numberless. He stands up; he sidles left and right of me; he saunters overhead in thousands of flakes that crowd and brighten. I look behind me: everywhere is snow.

His brush: a wisp of smoke from the treetops. They vanish, and make him disappear.

III

At times all I can see anymore is my shoes, punching holes in the crackly whiteness. Bold blue of laces, ochre of close-woven canvas, brown spots left there by the snow, which plops off as my steps pull me on, into eddies of light.

The painter named snow has done good work again, this morning. He's touched up what the branches already drew; and the sky runs toward me, laughing like a child. I tighten the big wool muffler around his neck.

LES NOMS DIVINS

I

Leur raisonnement, c'était que Dieu ne peut désirer que nous lui donnions un nom, car l'idée de nom suggère celle de sujet, de verbe, de prédicat, on va donc vouloir que Dieu soit ceci ou cela, on le cherchera pour ce faire dans une de nos perceptions, qui s'opposera à d'autres, on se battra pour l'une ou l'autre, on s'entredéchirera en son nom ! Un nom pour l'absolu, ce n'est pas la désignation, encore moins la célébration, c'est le piège que nous tend, hélas, le langage. Le nom de Dieu est le mal. Dès que Dieu a nom le blé brûle, on perce le cou de l'agneau.

Mais à peine avaient-ils conclu ainsi, banalement, que s'enflammait leur angoisse. Car, devant un champ de blé, et le nom du blé leur venant aux lèvres, ils craignaient, percevant la beauté du blé, son évidence, son absolu, d'avoir déjà un peu nommé Dieu, et ainsi d'avoir fait le mal. Dans leur regard sur le blé au soleil, le nom qu'il ne faut pas concevoir avait passé comme une ombre, et celle-ci, frémissante, la voici maintenant qui noircissait là-bas la pente du coteau, dans ses vignes, et l'eau étincelante du fleuve ! Tout ce qu'ils aimaient, et de façon si légitime, pourtant, leur était occasion de faute. Toute pensée leur était un risque, et toute conversation d'abord, avec ceux qu'ils aimaient surtout: car à s'aimer on s'exalte, on trouve divin ce qui est, on a désir de le dire tel. Les promenades dans la lumière du soir étaient redoutées, on n'en faisait guère que les yeux baissés, inquiets même de ces pierres trop bleues que le diable peut-être avait placées sur la route. La couche des amants était dangereuse. L'enseignement avait à se faire abstraction sans fin, rebutante, puisque faire allusion à

NAMING THE DIVINE

I

God can't want us to give him a name, they reasoned. The idea of names would call subjects, verbs, and predicates to mind; so people would prefer a God who's this or that. To pin him down, they'd favor only one of our viewpoints, which would contradict the others, and the opposing camps would tear each other to shreds—all in his name. A name doesn't label the absolute, much less exalt it; regrettably, it's a trap set for us by language. The name of God is evil itself. As soon as we give God a name, the wheat starts to burn, and we slash the lamb's neck.

But they'd hardly reached this trite conclusion, when their worries really flared up. Before a wheat field, say, the name of wheat would come to their lips; and the absolute presence, the beauty of wheat, would lead them to fear they'd named God somewhat—already committing an evil. Before the sunlit wheat, the name they mustn't conceive had shuddered through their gaze like a shadow; and now it blackened the vineyard on the hillside over there, and the river's sparkling flow. Everything they loved, no matter how rightly, might lure them into sin. Each thought posed a risk; but each conversation even more, especially with those they loved. After all, loving elates us: we feel the real has become divine, and long to say so. They dreaded walks in the evening light, and only undertook them with lowered eyes. They even suspected the stones along the road: those are too blue; maybe the devil put them there . . . The lovers' bed was dangerous. And teaching was intended to repel students, through endless

la rose, au vin, dans la beauté d'un poème, cela laissait entrevoir des choses qui, participant de l'être de Dieu, privaient l'esprit de ce bien qu'est dans les mots son absence.

Fallait-il ne plus regarder, par crainte de voir ? Ne toucher à quoi que ce soit sinon par le truchement d'instruments qui sachent mettre à distance, comme ces bras de métal à l'aide desquels les robots pénètrent le feu, le froid, ou l'extrêmement petit, ou le vide?

Leur solution fut d'écarter de leur vie plus encore ces occasions qu'ils n'avaient que trop d'aimer ceci ou cela du monde. Ils firent indéfiniment le vide dans leurs journées, dans leurs nuits. Ils le firent aussi dans leurs paroles. Ils renoncèrent aux arts qui représentent, et même à celui qui évoque et semblait grand de ne vouloir qu'évoquer, avec ses fiévreux et naïfs emportements d'enthousiasme. Ils renoncèrent à tout ce qu'ils pouvaient craindre sérieux, car le sérieux s'attarde à des affections, à des valeurs, à des souvenirs. Faute de pouvoir s'aveugler vraiment, se taire vraiment, ils organisèrent ce qui pouvait sembler des spectacles, mais de ceux auxquels on ne jette qu'un bref regard en passant, inintéressé, parce qu'on continue de vaquer à ses autres tâches. C'était sur la rive, de préférence la nuit. Des hommes déchargeaient de quelque bateau de grands coffres. Ils les empilaient sur le quai que trempaient des flaques. Ils les déplaçaient, lourds comme on sentait qu'ils étaient de grandes barres de fer qui remuaient dans leur être clos. Voila qui est « jouer à Dieu », disait-on. Il valait mieux jouer à Dieu que le vénérer car on vénère par métaphore, et la métaphore fragmente, et le fragmenté est la mort.

Ils résolurent de mourir, car Dieu, c'était trop pour vivre. D'aucuns se suicidèrent sans plus tarder. Beaucoup d'autres s'appesantirent dans une indifférence méfiante. Et ces derniers moururent

abstraction. Alluding to the roses or wine in a beautiful poem might unveil certain things that partake of God's nature, depriving the mind of that goodness his absence gives to words.

Should they avoid looking anymore, for fear of seeing? And not touch things at all, except with tools to keep them at bay? Like those metal arms robots use to probe heat, cold, a vacuum, or extreme tininess.

The world teemed with too many chances to love this or that. Their solution? Dismiss them from their lives, even more than before. They emptied their days and nights, indefinitely, and their words as well. They renounced the performing arts, even the one that merely wants to evoke, and whose greatness seemed to lie in precisely that; now they turned their backs on its naive, gushing transports. They rejected anything that threatened to turn serious, since when we're serious we dwell on our affections, our values, our memories. Because they couldn't go totally blind and mute, they organized what passed for performances—though only the sort you glance at blankly as you hasten by, intent on your own affairs. They staged them along the shore, preferably at night. Men would unload big chests from a boat; they'd pile them up on the dock, drenched with puddles. They'd haul the chests around, heavy with what you could tell were large, iron bars that rolled inside self-enclosed space. That's "playing God" for you, people would say. Playing God was better than revering him, because we venerate through metaphor; and metaphor splits into fragments, and what's fragmented is death.

They resolved to die, because God was too much for them to live. Some committed suicide, without delay. Many more sank into a wary indifference; they also died, when their time ran out. On this island,

aussi, leur heure venue. On voit les restes de leur civilisation dans cette île. Ce sont de beaux temples, bien qu'en ruines. D'admirables statues sont encore sur leurs parois, souriantes souvent, yeux décolorés, mains longues et souples. Certaines sont d'hommes et de femmes nus avec grande innocence dans leur maintien mais aussi quelque chose de bien triste, comme s'ils pressentaient ce qui allait advenir. Faut-il penser, quel paradoxe, que cet art était trop beau, apportait trop de joie ? Il apparaît en tout cas qu'il y eut un jour dans ces lieux un être de foi étrange et funèbre qui décida que l'humanité est coupable d'avoir autour de soi et en soi des objets que l'on puisse aimer, des êtres dont on puisse prendre avec bonheur les mains dans les siennes : sources dont on puisse boire l'eau fraîche. Dieu est davantage, s'écriait-il. Sans comprendre qu'à mettre le feu à tout il donnait encore à son dieu des noms, incendie, mort; et trahissait celui qui, peut-être, avait besoin que l'on inventât pour lui le bonheur; un dieu qui eût aimé partager son nom avec tout et rien sur la terre: étant alors le champ de blé, étant le soleil, étant la chevelure éparse dans la pénombre du lit, étant à l'infini les sautes du vent, le brin d'herbe.

II

Nous sommes descendus des hauteurs, vers le rivage. La chapelle est bâtie tout au bord de la plage, c'est en fait une simple hutte de pisé, avec une petite fenêtre que divise à la verticale un barreau de fer. L'herbe pousse abondamment tout autour, elle envahit même la porte, il faudra peiner un peu pour l'ouvrir. Un palmier étend son ombre précaire sur le toit, qui est de tuiles et réparé avec des branchages. Il est presque midi. Mon guide, mon ami, tourne la vieille clef dans la vieille serrure, et nous entrons. Dans la salle, rien qu'un sol de sable

you can see the remains of their civilization. Though in ruins, the temples are lovely. Statues, often smiling, still grace the walls—their eyes discolored, their hands long and willowy. Some are nudes, men and women with an air of signal innocence—but also a note of deep sadness, as if foreseeing what would come. Was this art too beautiful? Did it give them too much joy? What a paradox . . . At any rate, we gather that one day, in these precincts, a strange and funereal creed arose. It declared humans guilty of loving things, outward and inward; of contentedly taking other people's hands in their own: springs of cool water where they could drink. God is more than that, cried the defenders of the faith. Without grasping that when they burned the world to ash, they were still giving names to their god: fire, death. That maybe they had betrayed some other god, who needed us to invent happiness for him. A god who would have liked to share his name with all the earth: so he could be the field of wheat, and be the sun; could be the hair unloosed on the shadowy bed; could be the shifting winds, and the blade of grass—on and on into the infinite.

II

We walked down from the heights, and headed for the shore. The chapel, a simple adobe hut, is right at the edge of the beach. A vertical iron bar divides its small window. Grass runs riot around the place, even spilling under the door, so you have to pry it open. A palm spreads its teetering shade over the roof, built of tiles and patched with branches. The hour is almost noon. My guide, my friend, turns the old key in the old lock, and we step inside. Besides the floor of pale sand,

très clair, quelques oranges séchées, déjà presque bleues, poussées dans un coin, et en face de nous, posée à terre, on croirait abandonnée, une statue ou plutôt l'ébauche d'une statue. La tête du saint n'a pas même été commencée, en effet, on ne distingue dans ce billot de bois sombre que la forme du corps, que le sculpteur, dirait-on, voulait camper debout, une jambe en avant, le torse nu au-dessus d'un de ces longs pagnes qu'on voit aux porteurs d'eau ou aux scribes dans cette Égypte qui, certes, n'est pas si loin : là-bas au sud, seulement à deux ou trois jours de navigation incertaine, ces autres sables et palmeraies dont l'odeur est souvent perçue dans l'île où nous sommes, elle la grande île face au grand fleuve, elle la montagne qui entre le rien et le rien s'élève dans des nuées.

La tête du saint n'est pas commencée. Je prends pourtant le morceau de bois dans mes mains, je le soulève, il est assez lourd, je regarde ce qui est le plus avancé, dans ce travail d'il y a quelques jours mais peut-être aussi quelques siècles, ce sont les mains qui se rejoignent sur la poitrine, serrées sur ce qui semble une sphère, encore que celle-ci serait bien irrégulière, le sculpteur n'ayant pas cherché à évoquer le lisse et le plein d'un volume comme la géométrie en connaît. Même, je comprends vite que l'irrégularité n'a pas été crainte, peut-être même a-t-elle été tout à fait voulue. On dirait aussi que les doigts de cet être inconnu se crispent sur cette chose ; que la matière de celle-ci cède légèrement sous leur pression.

Je pose la statue, je lève les yeux, je regarde autour de moi dans la salle, rien d'autre pour retenir l'attention, si ce n'est la couleur qui s'écaille auprès des poutres de la charpente, là où l'eau s'infiltre aux heures de pluie, sans doute rares. Le battant a été presque tout à fait refermé, rien qu'un rayon mais intense, presque aveuglant, passe là

there's nothing in the room but some oranges shoved in a corner, so dried up they're almost blue; and facing us, placed on the ground, a statue. More like the rough outline of a statue, apparently left behind. The saint's head wasn't even begun: in this dark block of wood, you can only make out the shape of a body. I assume the sculptor meant for it to stand with one leg forward, its torso naked above a knee-length loincloth: the kind worn by water-bearers and scribes to the south, in Egypt, which isn't that far away—just two or three days of unpredictable sailing. The smell of those other dunes and palm groves often wafts to the island where we are: the big island across from the big river, a mountain rising out of nowhere into the clouds.

The saint's head isn't even begun. All the same, I hoist the chunk of wood with my hands—it weighs a good deal—to examine the part where some progress was made. The work on this piece might have been done several days ago; or just as well, several centuries ago. I note how the hands join together over the chest, holding what seems to be a sphere, though it's very uneven. The sculptor didn't try to depict the smooth fullness of a volume, as found in geometry. In fact, I quickly realize he didn't avoid that unevenness: that maybe it was just what he wanted. The unknown being's fingers also appear to clutch the object, so its surface yields a bit under their grip.

I set the statue down, and survey the room around me. There's nothing else in here to catch the eye, unless it's the paint peeling along the roof beams, where water must seep through when it rains—which happens rarely, no doubt. The shutter has been closed, almost entirely: a single ray of light, blindingly intense, slants between the wall

entre le bois sombre et le mur. Quant à mon guide, il est ressorti, je crois l'entendre qui parle avec quelques enfants au dehors.

J'ai vu ces enfants, tout à l'heure. Le plus grand sur sa bicyclette, mais un pied demeuré au sol, traînant une vieille savate, zigzagant près de ses amis. Et les deux ou trois autres si jeunes que l'un au moins va nu, dans la lumière. Leurs corps sont comme le bronze de statues que l'Égypte n'aurait pas eues, coloré comme il semble l'être par les feux d'un soleil couchant. Je me suis dit au passage qu'ils savent, eux; ou tout au moins n'ont pas tout à fait oublié encore.

and the dark wood. As for my guide, he's gone outside again; I think I hear him talking with some children out there.

I saw those children, just now. The oldest was riding his bike; dragging a foot along the ground in his worn-out shoe, he zigzagged next to several friends. They're so young that one of them, at least, goes naked in the light. Their bodies recall the statues of bronze Egypt never had, a bronze that seems tinged by fires of a setting sun. Passing by them, I said to myself: they know; or if they don't, they haven't completely forgotten.

LE TOMBEAU DE LEON-BATTISTA ALBERTI

Rêva-t-il son tombeau cette façade ?
Il pressentit la harpe dans la pierre
Et voulut que le son de ces arcatures
Se fît or sans matière, poésie.

Ne change rien,
Disait-il à son maître d'œuvre, sinon la mort
Ravagera les nombres, tu détruiras
« Toute cette musique », notre vie.

La façade est inachevée, comme toute vie,
Mais les nombres y sont enfants, qui y jouent, simples,
À être l'or dans l'eau où ils pataugent.

Ils se bousculent, ils se donnent des coups,
Ils crient, ils s'éclaboussent de lumière,
Ils se séparent en riant quand la nuit tombe.

ALBERTI'S TOMB

Did he dream of this facade as his tomb?
In stone, he carved the inkling of a harp,
And willed the sound of arcatures
To turn to poetry, to immaterial gold.

Don't change a thing,
He told his builder, or else the numbers
Will be gutted by death, and you'll destroy
"All this music," our life.

The facade is unfinished—just like every life.
But its numbers are simply children, playing
At being gold, in the water where they splash.

They tussle, they roughhouse, they whoop,
They splatter each other with light—and then,
At nightfall, they say good-bye with a laugh.

LE TOMBEAU DE CHARLES BAUDELAIRE

Je n'imagine rien, pour se pencher
Sur toi, que les mots quittent, le soir venu
De ton étonnement sur cette terre,
Que ceux, non sus de nous, de l'inconnue

Que tu as dite une Électre pensive
Qui essuyait ton grand front enfiévré
Et, « d'une main légère », dissipait
L'épouvante dans ton sommeil brûlé de fièvre.

Et tu la désignas mystérieusement
Parce qu'être compatissant est le mystère
Même, ce qui permit à ces trois lettres,

J, G, F, de s'accroître dans la lumière
Sur laquelle ta barque glisse. D'être pour toi
Le port enfin : ses portiques, ses palmes.

BAUDELAIRE'S TOMB

Words take leave of you in the evening
Of your bafflement, here on this earth;
To draw near you, I only need imagine
Those the unknown woman said, words

We can but guess. A pensive Electra,
You called her. Wiping your high,
Fevered brow with her "light hand,"
She cooled the horrors of your sleep.

You kept her a mystery, because
Compassion is the mystery itself.
And that is why these three letters,

J, G, F, have expanded in the light
That lifts your gliding boat. In the end,
They are your haven: its porticoes, its palms.

L'ARBRE DE LA RUE DESCARTES

Passant,
Regarde ce grand arbre et à travers lui,
Il peut suffire.

Car même déchiré, souillé, l'arbre des rues,
C'est toute la nature, tout le ciel,
L'oiseau s'y pose, le vent y bouge, le soleil
Y dit le même espoir, malgré la mort.

Philosophe,
As-tu chance d'avoir l'arbre dans ta rue,
Tes pensées seront moins ardues, tes yeux plus libres,
Tes mains plus désireuses de moins de nuit.

THE TREE ON DESCARTES STREET

Passer-by,
Look at this big tree. Look through it:
Maybe this tree is enough.

A street-tree, it's dirty and torn.
But still it's all of nature, all of the sky:
Where the wind blows, where birds alight,
Where the sun tells of hope, always the same
In spite of death.

Philosopher,
If you're lucky enough to have this tree in your street,
Your thoughts will come easier, your eyes will rove freer,
Your hands will reach out for less night.

L'INVENTION DE LA FLÛTE À SEPT TUYAUX

À un moment dans son dernier récit
Il commença, en ses mots effrayés,
À courir, comprenant que pesait sur lui
Une menace, en chacun d'eux croissante.

Comme si, des couleurs que dissocie
Le nom impénétrable de chaque chose,
Ou du ciel, qu'illimite le nom du vent,
Retombait une vague, sur sa vie.

Poète, la musique suffira-t-elle
À te sauver de la mort par le son
De cette flûte à sept tuyaux, que tu inventes ?

Ou n'est-ce là que ta voix qui s'essouffle
Pour que dure ton rêve ? Nuit, rien que nuit,
Ce froissement de roseaux sous la rive.

THE INVENTION OF THE SEVEN-PIPE FLUTE

At some point, in his final tale, he started
Racing through his frightened words.
In every syllable, a mounting threat
Overshadowed him.

As if—from the colors disjoined
By each thing's fathomless sound, or
From the sky unleashed by wind's name—
A wave toppled back, over his life.

Poet, will music suffice to save you
From death? Is that why you invented
The sound of this seven-pipe flute?

Or is it just your voice, so that your dream
Will last, even out of breath? Night, only night,
This rustle of reeds, down by the shore.

LE TOMBEAU DE GIACOMO LEOPARDI

Dans le nid de Phénix combien se sont
Brûlé les doigts à remuer des cendres !
Lui, c'est de consentir à tant de nuit
Qu'il dut de recueillir tant de lumière.

Et ils ont élevé, ses mots confiants,
Non le quelconque onyx vers un ciel noir
Mais la coupe formée par leurs deux paumes
Pour un peu d'eau terrestre et ton reflet,

O lune, son amie. Il t'offre de cette eau,
Et toi penchée sur elle, tu veux bien
Boire de son désir, de son espérance.

Je te vois qui vas près de lui sur ces collines
Désertes, son pays. Parfois devant
Lui, et te retournant, riante ; parfois son ombre.

LEOPARDI'S TOMB

So many fingers have been singed,
Sifting ashes in the phoenix nest;
But he could harvest all this light
Only by assenting to all this night.

And his trusting words never raised
Some onyx chalice to a blackened sky.
Their palms joined to cup your face,
Mirrored in earthly water, O moon,

His friend. He offers you this cup,
And you lean down, you consent
To drink from his yearning hope.

I see you roam beside him on these lonely hills,
His native land. At times you move ahead; you turn
Around to him and laugh. At times, you're his shadow.

MAHLER, *LE CHANT DE LA TERRE*

Elle sort, mais la nuit n'est pas tombée,
Ou bien c'est que la lune emplit le ciel,
Elle va, mais aussi elle se dissipe,
Plus rien de son visage, rien que son chant.

Désir d'être, sache te renoncer,
Les choses de la terre te le demandent,
Si assurées sont-elles, chacune en soi
Dans cette paix où miroite du rêve.

Qu'elle, qui va, et toi, qui vieillis, continuez
Votre avancée sous le couvert des arbres,
À des moments vous vous apercevrez.

Ô parole du son, musique des mots,
Tournez alors vos pas l'une vers l'autre
En signe de connivence, encore, et de regret.

MAHLER, *THE SONG OF THE EARTH*

She comes out; but night hasn't fallen yet,
Or else it's the moon that fills the sky.
She walks, but also melts away: nothing
Is left of her face—nothing but her song.

Desire to be, you must renounce yourself:
This is what the things of earth demand—
So trustingly, that each of them reflects
The shimmering peace of this dream.

She moves forward, and you grow old.
Keep advancing, under interwoven trees,
And you'll glimpse each other, now and then.

O music of words, utterance of sound,
Bend your steps toward each other as a sign
Of complicity, at last . . . and of regret.

LE TOMBEAU DE STÉPHANE MALLARMÉ

Sa voile soit sa tombe, puisque il n'y eut
Aucun souffle sur cette terre pour convaincre
La yole de sa voix de dire non
Au fleuve, qui l'appelait dans sa lumière.

De Hugo, disait-il, le plus beau vers :
« Le soleil s'est couché ce soir dans les nuées »,
L'eau à quoi rien n'ajoute ni ne prend
Se fait le feu, et ce feu le subjugue.

Nous le voyons là-bas, indistinct, agiter
À la proue de sa barque qui se dissipe
Ce que des yeux d'ici ne discernent pas.

Est-ce comme cela que l'on meurt ? Et à qui
Parle-t-il ? Et que reste-t-il de lui, la nuit tombée ?
Cette écharpe de deux couleurs, creusant le fleuve.

MALLARMÉ'S TOMB

His sail should be his tomb, since no
Breath on this earth could convince
The skiff of his voice to say no
To the river's summons of light.

Here, he said, is Hugo's loveliest verse:
"The sun has set, this evening, in the clouds."
Water lets nothing be added or removed:
It turns to fire; by that fire he's consumed.

We see him blurring, far away, as his boat
Fades from view. At its prow, what is he
Waving? We can't tell—not from here.

Is that how people die? And who's he talking to?
What will be left of him, when night comes on?
Plowing the river, this two-colored scarf.

À L'AUTEUR DE « LA NUIT »

Il entra dans sa tombe avant sa mort.
C'était sa ville de chaque soir mais dépeuplée.
Noire la grande porte. Quelques passants
Au loin, encore. Puis personne, dans la nuit.

Il suivit une rue, puis d'autres, d'autres.
Une charrette, une fois. Mais sans yeux
Le cocher, ni visage. Et à nouveau
Ne retentit que l'écho de ses pas.

Grilles qu'il secoua à des cours fermées,
Sonnettes éperdument, dont la rumeur
Se perdait dans les escaliers de maisons vides.

Il descendit des marches, vers un quai
Où un reste du fleuve coulait encore.
Il écouta le bruit se défaire du temps.

TO THE AUTHOR OF "NIGHT"

Before his death, he entered his tomb: it was
His city of each evening, though deserted now.
The portal was black. Far off, a few stragglers
Hurried away. Then no one, only night.

He sidled down this street, that street, then another.
Once, he even saw a cart; but the coachman
Had no eyes, had no face. And again, all he heard
Was his own footfall, echoing between the walls.

He shook the iron gates to sealed-off courts:
No one home. Frantically, he rang the bells;
But empty stairways swallowed every sound.

He went down steps to a landing by the river:
A thread of the stream still flowed. He listened
To that trickle, washing its hands of time.

SAN GIORGIO MAGGIORE

Se peut-il que derrière ces façades
Nobles comme l'enfance qui vint nue,
Il n'y ait qu'une suite de salles sombres,
L'une ouvrant sur une autre, à l'infini ?

Tel pourtant le malheur de l'Intelligible,
Son rêve prend la forme dans ses mains,
Mais que de soubresauts dans cette lumière !
L'artère de l'absence bat ici.

Et des mains se conjoignent, ce fut ce porche,
Mais pour brandir le fer d'un sacrifice.
L'agneau meurt au sommet de la symétrie,

Architecte, délivre de ce sang
L'espoir que dit la forme dans la pierre,
Le bien de la lumière est à ce prix.

SAN GIORGIO MAGGIORE

These facades are childhood at its birth:
Noble and nude. But what lies behind?
Nothing but a chain of somber rooms,
Link after link, stretching to infinity?

True, such is the Idea's mischance.
It dreams of form, but molded in its hands,
Light only moves in fits and starts.
Here, absence pulses like an artery.

Yes, hands are clasped above this portico—
And yet they wield the sword of sacrifice.
At symmetry's peak, the lamb must die.

Architect, deliver from this blood
The hope that form has uttered here in stone.
Light's blessing comes at that price.

SUR TROIS TABLEAUX DE POUSSIN

Sa tombe, me dit-on ? Mais c'est ce creux
Qu'il a laissé, sombre, dans le feuillage
De l'arbre où Apollon vieilli médite
Sur qui est jeune et donc est plus qu'un dieu.

Et c'est aussi la trouée de lumière
Dans la *Naissance de Bacchus*, quand le soleil
Prend l'espérance encore inentamée
Dans ses mains, et en fait le ciel qui change.

Sa tombe ? Ce que voit son regard sévère
Se défaire, au profond de l'*Autoportrait*
Dont le tain, qui aima son rêve, s'enténèbre :

Un vieil homme étonné, le soir venant,
Mais s'obstinant à dire la couleur,
Tard, sa main devenue pourtant chose mortelle.

ON THREE PAINTINGS BY POUSSIN

His tomb? they ask me. Well, it's the dark
Hollow he tucked in the foliage of a tree.
There, already old, Apollo meditates
On youth, a force no god can match.

It's also the light that pokes through clouds
In the *Birth of Bacchus*, when the sun
Scoops up our hope, still untried,
And molds it into ever-changing sky.

His tomb? It erodes before the stare
Of his stern eyes in the *Self-Portrait*:
Dimmed, its silvering tarnishes his dreams.

An old man, he is surprised. As evening falls,
He perseveres in saying color—even if it's late;
Even if his hand is now but a mortal thing.

ULYSSE PASSE DEVANT ITHAQUE

Qu'est-ce que ces rochers, ce sable ? C'est Ithaque,
Tu sais qu'il y a là l'abeille et l'olivier
Et l'épouse fidèle et le vieux chien,
Mais vois, l'eau brille noire sous ta proue.

Non, ne regarde plus cette rive ! Ce n'est
Que ton pauvre royaume. Tu ne vas pas
Tendre ta main à l'homme que tu es,
Toi qui n'as plus chagrin ni espérance.

Passe, déçois. Qu'elle fuie à ta gauche ! Voici
Que se creuse pour toi cette autre mer,
La mémoire qui hante qui veut mourir.

Va ! Garde désormais le cap sur l'autre
Rive basse, là-bas ! Où, dans l'écume,
Joue encore l'enfant que tu fus ici.

ULYSSES PASSES ITHACA

What's this pile of rocks and sand? Ithaca . . .
You know you'll find the bees, the ancient dog,
The olive tree, the faithful wife. But look:
The water glitters, black under your prow.

No, don't waste another glance: this coast
Is just your threadbare kingdom. You won't
Shake the hand of the man you are now—
You who've lost all sorrow, and all hope.

Sail on, disappoint them. Let the island slip by,
Off to port. For you, this other sea unrolls:
Memory haunts the man who wants to die.

Speed ahead. From this day on, set your course
For that low, huddled shore. There, in the foam,
Plays the child that you once were, here.

SAN BIAGIO, À MONTEPULCIANO

Voûtes, arches, colonnes : il savait bien
Vos façons de promettre sans tenir,
Et que votre âme autant que votre corps
Se refuse à des mains qui veulent prendre.

Quel leurre que l'espace ! Les architectes du ciel,
Ceux qui assemblent et désassemblent les nuées,
Offrent plus, à si vite décevoir,
Que les nôtres, qui n'échafaudent que des rêves.

Il rêva, cependant ; mais au jour dit
Il fit de la beauté meilleur usage,
Comprenant que la forme est pour mourir.

Et son œuvre, cette dernière : une monnaie
Dont les faces sont nues. De cette salle
Il a fait arc et flèche dans la pierre.

SAN BIAGIO, AT MONTEPULCIANO

Columns, arches, vaults: how he knew
The ways you promise but don't give;
And that your bodies, like your souls,
Always slip from our grasping hands.

Space is such a lure . . . Swift to disappoint,
As they raise and topple clouds, the sky's
Architects still offer more than ours,
Who only build a scaffolding of dreams.

He dreamed, all the same; but on that day,
He gave a better use to beauty's shapes:
He understood that form helps us die.

And this, his final work, is a coin
With both sides bare. He made in stone,
Of this great room, the arrow and the bow.

UNE PIERRE

Il voulut que la stèle
Où graver la mémoire de ce qu'il fut,
Ce soit une des plaques de safre clair
Qu'il remuait du pied, dans le ravin.

Leurs entailles, leurs mousses rouge sombre,
Ce désordre qui fait, indéchiffrable,
Que chacune est unique, bien que la même
Que toute autre : ce serait là son épitaphe.

Il rêva, il mourut. Où est sa tombe ?
Passant, si tu te risques sur ces pentes,
Percevras-tu les mots qu'il crut porter

Dans la pierre gélive ? Entendras-tu
Sa voix, parmi ces bruits d'insectes ? Pousseras-tu
D'un pied distrait sa vie dans plus bas encore ?

A STONE

For his stele, carved
With the memory of what he'd been,
He wanted those pale, sandstone slabs
Stubbed by his foot in the ravine.

Their russet lichens, scars and nicks—
The cryptic jumble that makes them each
The same, though each unique:
This would be his epitaph.

He dreamed. He died. Where is his tomb?
Passer-by, if you venture along these slopes,
Will you unearth the words he scrawled

On frost-split stone? Will you detect his voice
Below the insects' rasp? With a careless tread,
Will you push his life even further down?

LE TOMBEAU DE PAUL VERLAINE

Ce « peu profond ruisseau », où coule-t-il
Plus avant qu'en ses vers, qui savent bien
Que toute rive est proche, dans les joncs
Enchevêtrés du désir et du rêve ?

Juges, au soir, les mots !
Boue autant que lumière, vérité !
Lui ne l'oubliait pas, bien qu'irritant, futile,
Son propos tressautât de pierre en pierre.

Il fut humble, par fierté simple, il consentit
À n'être pour les autres qu'un miroir
Dont le tain dévasté filtrerait le ciel.

À eux de voir que le ciel fut en lui,
À son plus rouge à travers ces feuillages
Du soir, quand le roucoulement des ramiers s'enténèbre.

VERLAINE'S TOMB

Where does it flow, this "shallow stream,"
If not in his verses? How well they know
That every shore is close, entangled
In the rushes of dream and desire.

When evening falls, words are judges:
Mud as much as light, they are truth.
This he never forgot—even when his phrases,
Grating, futile, lurched from rock to rock.

He was humble, and simple out of pride.
For others, he agreed to be a mirror, nothing more:
His silvering, pocked and worn, filters the sky.

Now they, in turn, must see that sky in him—
Deepening to red through darkened leaves,
When twilight shrouds the cooing of the doves.

UN SOUVENIR D'ENFANCE DE WORDSWORTH

Comme, dans *Le prélude,* cet enfant
Qui va dans l'inconscient de la lumière
Et avise une barque et, entre terre et ciel,
Y descend, pour ramer vers une autre rive,

Mais voit alors s'accroître, menaçante,
Une cime là-bas, noire, derrière d'autres,
Et prend peur et retourne à ces roseaux
Où de minimes vies murmurent l'éternel,

Ainsi ce grand poète aura poussé
Sa pensée sur une heure calme du langage,
Il se crut rédimé par sa parole.

Mais des courants prenaient, silencieux,
Ses mots vers plus avant que lui dans la conscience,
Il eût peur d'être plus que son désir.

A CHILDHOOD MEMORY OF WORDSWORTH'S

As in *The Prelude*, when the child sets forth,
Unconscious as the light, and spots a boat;
And pushes off, between the earth and sky,
To row toward another shore. But then,

Over there, he sees an ominous black crag,
Looming taller and taller behind the rest;
And in his dread, hurries back into the reeds,
Where miniscule lives eternally hum.

So this great poet must have embarked
His thought on a tranquil hour of language,
And believed himself redeemed by speech.

But other currents, silent, drove his words
Ahead of what his mind could apprehend,
Till he feared he'd overtopped his desire.

REMARQUES SUR L'HORIZON

Parlons de l'horizon, mes amis, de quoi pourrions-nous parler d'autre ?

Toujours nous parlons de lui, ou plutôt en lui. Quand nous formons des projets, quand nous aimons.

Quand nous aimons, car aimer, un être, un chemin, une œuvre, c'est voir que cette ligne là-bas, si loin à l'avant, cette ligne toute lumière, est tout autant ici même à les traverser, les retraverser, comme sur la plage la mer vient et revient dans le sable, y soulevant puis y laissant retomber l'algue remuante, la vie obscure.

Ligne de là-bas et ligne de par ici, chacune à jeter l'écume de l'inconscient sous nos pas, phrase qui étincelle de glisser à la crête de cette vague qui se gonfle comme une nuit, puis s'écroule puis à nouveau se soulève.

Je prends ce chemin, il est étroit, il s'enfonce entre deux petites buttes, des arbres l'enveloppent aussi, se resserrent autour de moi, au-dessus de moi, j'ai bonheur à le savoir familier, avec ces mille vies de sa profondeur qui se sont habituées à moi. Mais plus bas que les pépiements, les ébrouements, les envols, ce son léger mais ininterrompu que j'entends, c'est le « là-bas » des collines de l'horizon qui, bien qu'invisible, m'accompagne. Tenant cet instant présent, cet instant d'ici, en ses mains que j'aperçois, bleues ou ocres rouge, dans une déchirure des pins et des petits chênes.

REMARKS ON THE HORIZON

Let's talk about the horizon, my friends—what else could we talk about?

We always talk about it—or in it, we might say. When we make plans, when we love.

When we love: because loving a being, a path, a work, is seeing that this line over there, so far ahead—this line made of light—is right here, just as well; that it crosses them over and over, like the surf when it slides back and forth on the sand, lifting the restless algae's hidden life, dropping it again.

The line of over there, the line of right here: each throws the foam of the unconscious mind beneath our steps, the sparkling phrase that glides to the breaker's crest—the wave swelling upward like a night, then crumbling to rise again.

I take this path: narrowly wedging its way between two stumpy mounds. The trees enfold it, too; they crowd around me, above me. I'm happy it's all so familiar; the thousand lives teeming in these depths have gotten used to me. But lower than the chirps, the flutters, the swoops, I hear a soft, continuous hum: the "over there" of the hills on the horizon, my companion, though invisible. Who holds the present instant, the moment of here, in those hands I glimpse, blue or reddish ochre: a gash between the scrub oaks and the pines.

Avec le ciel au-dessus d'ici pour me rappeler que le ciel est également de là-bas, qu'il peut voir par dessous la ligne où, pour nous ici, ce qui est a cessé d'être visible.

Et la couleur, parmi nous, comme ce secret qui est donc le sien.

Et le cri de cet oiseau qui reprend, qui est un appel. Sans doute vient-il de cet autre monde, il en rapporte l'or, quelque paille, au plus creux de son nid que l'on ne voit pas.

Et lumière de l'horizon cette eau qui tarde à s'évaporer, Dieu sait pourquoi, dans les flaques de sous nos pieds.

Dieu ? C'est-à-dire l'averse qui a choisi de tomber ici. Elle qui aurait pu tomber un peu plus loin dans ce petit bois : en cela le hasard, en cela divine.

Qui a pensée de l'horizon n'a pas de dieu : ces lointains lui suffisent, qui glissent du bas du ciel comme une eau sur les signes que trace ce petit enfant dans le sable.

Et cette eau se gonfle soudain, la vague efface les signes, c'est la fin de l'après-midi, l'enfant remonte du bruit de fond de la mer parmi à nouveau des voix, et de grands corps dénudés.

Horizon comme la pierre que je retire de la vase, avec dans ses creux l'odeur du sel.

With the sky above me here, so I'll recall the sky is equally over there, that it can see beneath the line where—viewed from here—we lose sight of all that is.

And color, this secret among us, is actually the horizon's.

And the call of this bird, who repeats it like an appeal. No doubt he comes from that other world, bringing back its gold: a piece of straw at the bottom of his nest, hidden from view.

And the horizon's light is this water—evaporating late, God knows why—in the puddles under our feet.

God? A shower that chose to fall here. It could have fallen a little ways on, in that copse of woods: that's why it's happenstance; that's why it's divine.

Whoever has thought of the horizon has no need of any god: he's content with these distances, which slide from below the sky like water on the marks this little child is tracing in the sand.

The water swells all of a sudden, and the wave wipes the marks away. It's the end of the afternoon. The child comes up from the sounding sea among voices again, and large naked bodies.

Horizon, like the stone I pull from the silt, the smell of salt in all its crevices.

Horizon dans le mot que je vois briller sous les autres, quand l'inconscient à sa marée haute vient laver d'eau claire les phrases que j'ai posées juste à sa limite, pour voir. Algues soulevées et qui retombent, paroles qui se défont mais avec à leur surface, un instant, la brume de sel d'une eau qui est peut-être le ciel.

Les mots n'offrent le plein de leur sens que si c'est « là-bas », à un horizon, que nous contemplons ce qu'ils disent. Ici nous voyons trop en détail, la pensée se loge dans des aspects trop nombreux, s'y déploie en trop de formules : et tout est ainsi livré au désir de posséder, de comprendre. Là-bas le tout prime sur les parties, les choses en redeviennent des êtres.

Comme chez Proust quand il voit sous le ciel « les clochers de Martinville ». Et c'est toute son existence à venir qui en est affectée, déjà. C'est avec la mémoire de ces êtres de l'horizon qu'il va en regarder d'autres qui, eux, ne sont que d'ici : cherchant cet or, leur présence au loin, dans le vaste nouveau creuset.

Le bleu des lointains dans les mots aussi, comme le sens rêvé dans la chose dite.

Je crois que je dois à peu près tout à des horizons de mes premières années. Horizons soit lointains soit proches, soit ouverts, sous de grands nuages, soit retirés dans la boucle de la rivière aux eaux sombres.

Et avec ma plus grande dette — ce mot, parce que je sais qu'il faudra bien restituer, au monde du dernier jour, ce qu'eau et feu, et

Horizon, in the word I see that shines beneath the others, when the clear tide of the unconscious washes over them. I had set some phrases at its edge, to take a look. Algae buoyed up and tilting back, words that break apart . . . but on their surface, for an instant, this salty mist of water that may be the sky.

Words offer their full meaning only when we observe what they say "over there," on a horizon. Here, we see too much detail; our mind bogs down in too many byways, marshals too many phrases—so everything is bent to our will to possess, to comprehend. Over there, the whole prevails over its parts, and things become beings again.

As in Proust, when he sees "the steeples of Martinville" beneath the sky; and already, they affect his whole future existence. With these beings from the horizon in his memory, he'll scrutinize others who're only from here: seeking that gold, their far-off presence, in the vast new crucible.

The blue of distance also in our words, like the meaning dreamed in what was said.

I think I owe almost everything to the horizons of my early years. Horizons, far-off or near . . . open, under full-blown clouds . . . or withdrawn, in the darkened waters of the river's bow.

And I owe my greatest debt—that word, because I'm aware we'll have to return, to the world of the last day, what water and fire, and sky

ciel et terre, nous donnent — envers un lieu de si près de moi que j'aurais pu, si j'avais été un autre, décider qu'il était l'ici, l'ici même. Car c'était le sommet d'une longue colline basse, à rien qu'une heure de marche : où un certain grand arbre, à contre-jour sous le ciel, était assez distant pour se signifier absolu et cependant assez proche pour paraître un point de ce monde. Que l'on parvienne à son pied, dans la chaleur de l'après-midi, déclinante, et il ne serait pas trop tard pour découvrir d'en dessous ses grandes branches la vallée jusqu'en cet instant inconnue et la maison familière.

Il est si facile de se mettre à mal rêver, quand l'horizon est trop loin ! Ou quand il est tout à fait bas sous les buissons d'une vaste plaine ou, pire, quand à bonne distance il enchevêtre des collines peu élevées où jouent des ombres et des rayons avec ici ou là un champ de vive couleur. Si autres que les nôtres sont alors son étincelance, ses flaques, ses restes de nuit incompréhensibles dans ce qui semble des failles ! On peut imaginer qu'il n'est pas une ligne mais un pays, avec un peu de celui-ci en deçà, de notre côté, et un peu de l'autre. Pays dont les choses, les habitants, que l'on aperçoit avec des jumelles, sont, d'évidence, occupés à une vie tout à eux, une vie ni d'ici ni d'ailleurs, ni du monde connu ni des mondes de l'inconnu. Qui sont ces êtres? Nos chemins ne mènent plus jusqu'à eux. Et leurs chemins à eux ne vont guère loin, de l'autre côté, là où c'est notre pays d'ici que probablement nous retrouverions à mesure si nous allions par là-bas, traversant sans le voir l'espace où l'autre pays se situe.

Le pays de l'horizon ! Ces caravanes qui cheminent entre notre terre et une autre. Ces fuites en Égypte, dans nos jumelles, qui passent

and earth have given us—to a place so nearby that if I'd been somebody else, I might have decided this was here, was here itself. It was the top of a long, low hill, only an hour's walk away, where a tall tree was backlit by the sky. The tree was far away enough to mean the absolute, but close enough to seem like a point in this world. If you reached its trunk, in the ebbing heat of afternoon, you would still have time to discover, from underneath its sturdy limbs, the valley unknown till this moment, and the familiar house.

It's so easy to start dreaming badly, when the horizon is too far. Or when it's buried under bushes, on some enormous plain. Or worse, when at a fair remove, it tangles the low-lying hills; or shuffles shadows and sun with the occasional bright-hued field. Its glints and puddles, its baffling dregs of night in what could pass for rifts, are so different then from ours. We could imagine it isn't a line but a country—which overlaps with ours, and straddles the other side, too. A land where the things and inhabitants we spy through our binoculars are clearly plunged in a life all their own, a life neither here nor there—not in the world we know, but not in worlds unknown. Who are these beings? Our trails don't lead all the way to them; and theirs peter out before long, on that other side. Over there, we'd probably find our country from over here—as soon we crossed the space, without seeing it, where that other country lies.

Land of the horizon . . . Those caravans that snake between some other earth and ours. Those flights into Egypt, through our binoculars,

de l'autre côté d'une longue dune pour reparaître plus loin. Cette insuffisance désespérante des jumelles. À peine un point lumineux les visages là-bas. On peut même en venir à croire que ce ne sont pas des visages, tant de rayons émanant d'eux, se heurtant à d'autres ! Peut-être des masques d'or. Peut-être des yeux qui se sont accrus dans les visages jusqu'à effacer le dessin qui même là-bas réduit ceux-ci à ce que nous sommes.

Une définition du langage: un ici qui respire et expire l'ailleurs, méduse aux dimensions d'une mer qui serait le monde.

L'écriture de poésie ? La terre de sous nos pas mais trempée comme après l'orage, creusée par de grandes roues qui ont passé, se sont éloignées. Terre toute ornières dont de brèves lueurs remontent.

Je rencontre la flaque, je m'arrête, je lève les yeux du chemin, j'entends le bêlement d'un agneau au loin, sous les nuages qui sont maintenant immobiles.

Une barrière grince, et c'est presque l'étincelance de la rose en soi. Celle du jardin interdit, gardé par un perroquet aux yeux sans lumière.

Dans le récit de Melville le voyageur dont celui-ci dit qu'il s'est mis en route, de Pittsfield vers Mount Greylock, par fascination pour une vitre qui à des heures s'enflamme sur son horizon quotidien. Heureux ceux qui vivent là, pense-t-il. Et il arrive à cette maison, il en pousse la barrière, entre dans une salle, voit à sa croisée une jeune fille qui regarde avec grand désir sa maison à lui, loin là-bas dans son autre

that file behind a sprawling dune, to reemerge farther along. These binoculars are woefully inadequate. The faces over there are just dots of light, at best. You could end up thinking they aren't faces at all, they give off so many clashing rays. Maybe gold masks. Maybe eyes grown so big they've blotted out the faces, whose outline—even over there—reduces them to what we are.

A definition of language: a here that breathes the elsewhere in and out, a medusa as large as a sea—which would be the world.

Writing poetry? The earth under our feet: soggy after a storm, and slashed by big wheels that have lumbered by. An earth all rutted, that gives off momentary gleams.

I come to the puddle; I stop and look up from the path. I hear a lamb bleating far away, under clouds that have now stood still.

A gate creaks, and it's almost the shimmer of the rose as such. Of the garden that's off-limits, guarded by a parrot with lightless eyes.

The traveler in Melville's story, who sets out from Pittsfield and heads toward Mount Greylock, entranced by a windowpane that flares, at certain hours, on his everyday horizon. How happy they are who live there, he thinks . . . And on reaching the house, he goes through the gate and enters a room, where he sees a young girl at the window. With longing, she looks at his own house, far over there in

monde. Pourquoi repart-il alors ? Par sympathie, par amour. Ne fait-il pas un grand don, peut-être le don suprême ? Il offre de ne pas éteindre en son illusoire foyer cette minime espérance dont il comprend qu'elle est le seul bien au moment où il y renonce.

Des peintres humanisent ainsi des paysages dont il se peut que nous ne comprenions pas tout de suite pourquoi ils nous retiennent, pour le reste de notre vie.

Et quand soudain le là-bas nous manque parce qu'ici c'est la neige, la brusque et pleine neige avec du vent pour en remuer la lumière, voici qu'enfin l'horizon est avec nous, nous le touchons, nous le traversons et retraversons à l'aveuglette, nous en buvons l'air frais, c'est le bonheur de la neige.

Horizon, un mot que pourtant je n'aime pas, j'en voudrais un autre. Un qui, de son rebord escarpé, tendrait la main à notre parole pour qu'elle grimpe vers lui, dans l'invisible. Un qui favoriserait parmi nous le peintre de paysage, lui assurant l'avenir dont la terre a besoin et qu'elle espère et qu'elle mourra peut-être de voir se briser un jour, coupe qui a roulé auprès d'elle.

another world. Why does he leave again? Out of sympathy; out of love. Doesn't he bestow a great gift—perhaps the greatest of all? He doesn't snuff out her faint glimmer of hope in its make-believe home. And as soon as he relinquishes that hope, he understands it is the only thing worth having.

That's how some painters humanize landscapes: at first glance, we may not grasp why they will keep their hold on us for the rest of our lives.

And all of a sudden, we miss the over-there, because it's snowing right here: a head-on, full-flurried snowfall, with wind to stir up the light; and now, at last, the horizon is with us. We touch it; we cross it at random, back and forth; we drink its fresh air. This is the happiness of snow.

Horizon—though I don't care much for that word; I'd rather have a different one. A word that would reach out a hand from its craggy ridge as our own words climb toward it, into the invisible. A word that would favor the landscape-painter among us, pledging him the future earth hopes for, and needs. She might even die if she saw it break someday, like a cup rolled alongside her.

UNE VARIANTE DE LA SORTIE DU JARDIN

Cette imagination, insistante. Un homme et une femme vont sous des arbres qui par endroits sont très proches les uns des autres, avec même des branches emmêlées dès presque le sol, si bien que ces deux êtres très beaux, très jeunes ont hésité, plusieurs fois, à s'engager dans ces frêles bruits odorants de feuilles froissées. Ils ont regardé autour d'eux, ils ont paru choisir de changer de route, mais c'est aussi qu'il est tôt encore, la matinée n'est guère avancée et déjà les arbres se clairsèment, leurs branches se font moins basses, l'orée est proche, bientôt franchie. Voici devant nous des régions de collines douces, d'un vert un peu doré, où il est aisé de penser que de petits lacs se cachent mais sans embarcations sur leurs eaux tranquilles. D'évidence, ce grand pays est désert, en sa belle lumière qui ne cesse pas de s'accroître.

Ils vont, ces deux, il leur arrive de traverser encore de petits bois, même ils s'y arrêtent parfois, se tournant du coup l'un vers l'autre, et vus de loin comme ils sont alors, entre le dernier arbre et le vaste ciel, c'est comme s'ils se parlaient, la jeune femme étendant son bras vers on ne sait où, à des horizons. Puis ils repartent mais ne sont-ils pas tout de même toujours ici, on pourrait croire immobiles ? Tant ce ciel et ces arbres, et ces eaux au loin, pressenties, cela pourrait être un tableau, une de ces toiles à dominante vert sombre qu'un peintre de vers 1660, un héritier de Poussin, un ami de Gaspard Dughet, aurait pu substituer au monde si du fond de ces années mystérieuses des vents avaient surgi comme ils auraient dû, pour disperser sous nos pas les feuilles restées du long hiver.

LEAVING THE GARDEN: A VARIANT

The imagination keeps insisting . . . A man and a woman walk under trees which in places are dense, their branches raddled almost to the ground. They're so thickset that these two beings—very beautiful and young—have balked several times before those faint, fragrant rustlings of crumpled leaves. They've peered around, as though they'd rather go by a different route. We should also observe that it's still early in the morning; and already the trees are thinning out, their limbs higher up on their trunks. The edge of the woods draws near, and soon we've passed beyond it. Before us unfolds an expanse of gentle hills, verdant with a tinge of gold, where you'd readily assume small lakes might be hidden—though without any boats on their placid waters. This wide-open country, with its radiant light that grows and grows, is clearly uninhabited.

The two of them walk on. From time to time, they stray through other copses; they even linger in them for a while, turning to each other when they do. Seen from afar, between a final tree and the enormous sky, they appear to be conversing. The young woman stretches out her arm toward who knows where, toward a horizon. And then they set off again . . . but even so, aren't they still here? You could almost believe they're motionless. This sky and these trees, with the lakes we sense in the distance, seem so much like a picture: one of those canvases, cast in a key of dark green, that a painter of 1660 or so, a successor of Poussin and a friend of Gaspard Dughet, might have substituted for the world—if winds had blown up from those unfathomable years, as they should have, to sweep the long winter's final leaves from our path.

Un tableau. Dans la forme des épaules, des bras, ces lignes qui fermement se dégagent comme lorsqu'un peintre travaille, et presque trop de vive couleur dans les chevelures ou sur les belles chairs libres, et dans les feuillages aussi, dans les fruits qu'on y aperçoit : oui, un tableau parce que je sais bien qui sont pour moi cet homme et cette femme qui passent ainsi devant nous, sur cette terre sinon déserte. C'est Ève et Adam après ce qu'on a pu dire la Faute. Ils sont chassés du jardin d'Éden, ils le traversent sans hâte, car le temps n'a pas commencé encore. Rien que les heures du ciel d'été dans ce pays sans chemins où la lumière seule décide, séparant en riant les couleurs qui jouent avec trop d'ardeur, se penchant pour en relever une qui est tombée, qui s'étonne.

Adam, Ève ? Ils ont tout un jour à errer ainsi sur la terre, après quoi, vers la fin de l'après-midi, quand le soleil baissera, soudain visible, les grilles apparaîtront au bout d'une longue, très longue allée de sable et le vent se sera levé, le ciel sera rouge, vers l'ouest, et il y aura dans les arbres des cris d'oiseaux de nouvelle sorte. La nuit attendra au-delà du seuil entrouvert, les deux proscrits y consentiront, ils s'éloigneront dans ces ombres, mais pour l'instant ils ne savent que cet instant, justement, cet intemporel instant présent des images. Une voix a-t-elle troué le ciel, à quelque heure avant ce matin paisible ? Des mots dans ce qui n'était que bruit dans les eaux et dans les feuillages, l'éclair d'une étoffe pourpre au travers de ces demi-teintes ? Ils ne s'en souviennent pas, ils n'y pensent pas.

Ils vont, simplement. Et parfois je ne les vois plus, mais non parce que le chemin qu'ils ont suivi me les cache. C'est plutôt que mon attention a été requise autrement, et ailleurs, et déjà à trois ou quatre reprises.

Je dois dire que partout sur ces terres d'ici le plus grand silence

A picture. In the form of the shoulders, the arms; in these lines that stand out firmly when a painter plies his trade. And the colors, almost too vivid in the hair, or the shapely untrammeled flesh—in the foliage, too, and the fruits we notice hanging there. Yes, a picture: since I'm well aware who they are for me, the man and woman who saunter past us, on an otherwise deserted earth. They're Adam and Eve, after what's been called Original Sin. They're being driven from the Garden of Eden, which they cross unhurriedly, since time still hasn't begun. It's nothing but the hours of a summer sky, in this trackless country where the light alone decides: laughing, she separates the colors that play too rough; or leans down to pick one up who's taken a tumble, to his surprise.

Adam, Eve? They have an entire day to amble like this on the earth—and then, when the sun sinks low, visible all of a sudden in the late afternoon, iron railings will appear at the end of a long, straight walkway of sand. The wind will rise, the sky will redden in the west, and the trees will stir with bird-cries never heard before. Beyond the open threshold, night will await these two exiles: they will consent to wander off into the dark. But for the moment, all they know is precisely this moment: the timeless present of images. Did a voice rend the sky, at some hour before this tranquil morning? Were there words in what was merely the water's babble, the whispering of leaves? A thunderbolt of crimson cloth, against these half-tone hues? They don't remember; they don't give any of this a thought.

They simply stroll along. And sometimes I lose sight of them, but not because the path they've taken blocks them from my view. No, it's just that my attention has focused elsewhere, three or four times so far.

I should note that over all this landscape, the greatest silence pre-

règne. Le lointain jacassement d'une pie, des meuglements on ne sait où dans les prés, les rebonds d'une pierre qui se détache d'une falaise et roule dans un ravin, rien de tout cela n'en trouble la paix, au contraire ces rumeurs du monde visible lui donnent profondeur, l'élargissent, le clarifient : comme le fait aussi la chaleur qui s'accroît, elle également, mais non sans un peu de brise. Et j'aime ce silence mais voici que je dois comprendre que désormais il m'inquiète autant qu'auparavant il me rassurait. Comme si un certain son que j'ai entendu était d'une autre nature que ce ruisseau, par exemple, qui près de nous n'en finit jamais de se briser à ses rives.

Un son. Qui a paru venir de plus loin mais aussi de plus près de moi que tous ces bruits irréguliers et sans conséquences. Et qu'aussi bien je n'ai pu comprendre, en son étonnante brièveté. Était-il quelque chose de seulement musical, l'écho d'une petite flûte des plaines d'une autre terre, était-ce une voix humaine ? J'écoute. Et ces deux êtres là-bas ont reparu, je les vois qui, oui, maintenant, se parlent mais vite décident, me semble-t-il, d'oublier qu'eux aussi ont entendu. Surpris, encore indécis peut-être, ils reprennent leur marche dans ce midi, déjà, où les ombres du matin, qui avaient de la transparence, vont se faire celles du soir.

Heures de l'après-midi, toujours les plus lentes du jour, les plus troublantes aussi puisque l'horizon se rapproche, les couleurs changent. Je regarde ces deux êtres que j'imagine, je vais par le même chemin, je pense à l'éternité et au temps, à la beauté des corps, à celle des gestes, que sais-je ?

Et voici qu'un buisson vient de frémir, devant eux. Des branches y ont bougé, comme si quelqu'un s'était caché là pour les voir et ne s'était enfui qu'à la dernière seconde. Quelqu'un ? Oui, car les

vails. A magpie's faraway chatter, a lowing somewhere in the meadows, a dislodged rock bouncing off a cliff and rolling down a ravine—none of that ruffles the calm. Just the opposite: these rumors of the visible world deepen the peace, enlarge and clarify its scope; and so does the mounting heat—the heat as well, though not without a languid breeze. And I love this silence; but here I have to admit it's started to trouble me, as much as it reassured me before. As if a certain sound I'd heard was of another nature than this nearby stream, say, which never ceases to shatter against its banks.

A sound. Which seemed to come from farther off, but also from closer by, than all these random, uneventful noises. And which I've also failed to grasp, in its startling briefness. Was it just a musical note, the echo of a little flute from distant plains? Was it a human voice? I listen. And those two figures over there have reappeared: yes, I see them now, talking it over but quickly agreeing—so I gather—to forget they heard something, too. Nonplussed—and maybe still doubtful—they wend their way again through what is already noon; and where the morning's shadows, which had been somewhat transparent, will become the shades of dusk.

Afternoon hours, always the slowest of the day—the most disturbing, too, since the horizon looms nearer, and colors change. I look at these two beings I imagine, and now I'm walking with them down the path. I think of eternity and time, of the beauty of bodies, of gestures—who knows what?

And then a bush quakes, right in front of them: its twigs have moved, as if someone had been crouching there to spy on them, and hadn't bolted till the last split-second. Someone? Yes, because animals

bêtes ne fuient pas de cette façon, qui restent dans leur ici et leur maintenant comme se rabat le rameau qu'écarte notre passage. Quelqu'un qui va courir, dans l'ailleurs, s'allonger dans l'herbe, se relever brusquement, courir encore, mais s'arrêter alors, paraître réfléchir, revenir. Quelqu'un ? Encore que de bien peu de poids, et très agile, très souple. Est-il la voix qui appelait de l'autre côté du visible, la petite flûte qui y rêvait ? Oui, c'est bien un enfant qui rôde ainsi, nu, inconscient de soi, dans ces solitudes.

Et qui revient, en effet. Car dans ce jour un moment étale puis qui baisse je sais bien que je le retrouverai trois ou quatre fois encore sur le passage de l'homme et de la femme, anxieux de les voir, désireux d'en être vu et tout autant effrayé de l'être. Il s'était laissé devancer, il les a rejoints, peut-être même, à la fin, auront-ils entrevu ses grands yeux sauvages fixés sur eux : un instant, avant que sur ce regard peut-être bouleversé le feuillage ne se referme.

Qu'il est difficile de se parler ! Le silence ? Mais c'est de l'eau, une surface où plonger le bras pour ce qui brille à son fond, sur le sable clair où passent des ombres ; et atteindra-t-on jamais ce que l'on voudrait saisir, je crains que non, une diffraction mystérieuse se joue de nous, irrésistiblement notre main se voit écartée de l'objet de notre désir. — Ils vont, l'un près de l'autre, l'après-midi se fait elle aussi cette brillance et ces ombres, je les vois un moment appuyés contre un rocher, ils se parlent. Sont-ils seuls ? Il y a du mouvement dans cette immobilité, l'étoffe claire du ciel du soir frissonne dans le vent qui se lève.

Je pense à la dernière fois, après combien d'autres, comment savoir, où cet enfant s'est retrouvé auprès d'eux, les épiant, prêt à se jeter à leurs pieds mais réfrénant ce désir, pourquoi ? A-t-il compris que

don't flee like that; they stay in their here and now, like a branch that swings back after we've passed. Someone who'll scurry off and lie down on the grass, who'll jump up and run again—but then he'll pause, think it over, and return. Someone? Even though he's nimble, lithe, and hardly weighs a thing. Is he the voice that called from the other side of the visible, the little flute I heard dreaming there? Yes, only a child would prowl like that, naked and artless, in this solitary place.

And in fact, he does return. In this daylight, becalmed for a moment before it lowers, I know I'll spot him several times more along the trail, eager to watch the man and woman—wanting to be seen, and yet afraid. He had let them file ahead of him awhile, but now he catches up with them. In the end, maybe they'll even glimpse his big, wild eyes staring through the foliage: only an instant, before the leaves snap back on his gaze—stunned, perhaps.

It's not easy to speak with each other . . . And silence? Silence is water, a surface where we plunge our arm for what glitters at the bottom, on the bright sand where shadows drift. Will we ever reach what we long to grasp? I'm afraid not. A mysterious diffraction gets the best of us; and hard as we resist, our hand is pushed away from what we desired. —They walk on, side by side; the afternoon is also dappled by that shining, that shade. I see them leaning for a while against a rock, talking to each other. Are they alone? There's movement in this immobility: the sky's clear cloth shudders in the evening wind.

I think of the last time—after how many others, who can tell?—when the child crept up to spy on them, ready to throw himself at their feet. He curbed his longing—but why? Did he understand it was

c'était là, et tout de suite, que tout allait prendre fin et a-t-il, de ce fait, désiré davantage encore puis renoncé avec d'autant plus de chagrin ou de joie sombre, après quoi il reprit son errance dans l'éternel ? Je me demande si c'est avant ou après ce jour qu'il a ramassé le roseau, touché le bruit, inventé le son, introduit dans la vie de la douleur et de l'espérance. Je me demande aussi pourquoi je me préoccupe de la peinture, ou plutôt de l'image dans la peinture : cette eau où ce qui est semble une seconde fois s'offrir mais rien qu'en reflet désormais, sans beaucoup de frémissement dans la forme qui se dilue dans des jeux de lumière et d'ombres.

there, right away, that everything would end? Is that what spurred his desire, so he renounced it with even greater grief, or darker joy, to rove through eternity once more? I wonder if it was before or after this day that he picked up the reed, touched off a noise, and invented sound, instilling our life with something of sorrow and something of hope. I wonder as well why I'm so absorbed by painting, or rather the image in painting: this water where the real is offered up a second time—but from now on, only as reflection, its shape scarcely rippling as it dilutes in the play of shadow and light.

UNE AUTRE VARIANTE

Ils fuyaient, le drap de la malédiction plaquait ses éclairs et sa pluie contre leurs corps. Sous leurs pieds nus la terre s'était faite cailloux blessants, boue glissante, racines dangereuses. Leurs jambes s'enfonçaient dans des trous dont il leur fallait s'arracher. Ce garçon tenait cette fille par la main, par là passait déjà en lui et aussi en elle quelque chose de plus que l'étonnement et la peur. Puis il y eut ce cri, elle est tombée, le sang coule déjà le long de sa jambe gauche, un rouge nouveau dans le monde, et lui, il l'aide à se relever mais la cheville ne porte plus, il faut qu'Ève prenne appui sur son bras pour boiter vers l'inconnu devant eux, dans l'inconnu autour d'eux, sous l'inconnu du ciel noir. La nuit est là, en effet, et comment avancer, d'autant qu'à chaque pas la souffrance se fait plus grande ? Des pas de plus en plus difficiles dans le chaos du dehors qui s'étend à un autre au sein de ces deux qui vont sans rien savoir ni vouloir sinon aller ailleurs, aller loin. Des pas ? Moins des pas que des heurts à d'épaisses branches dans la pénombre, avec de l'eau pour se déverser d'un coup sur le bras qui cherche en avant sous les feuilles. Et moins désirer passer au travers de ces fourrés qui semblent sans fin ni faille que renoncer à le faire, ne plus savoir ce vent, ces averses, oublier cette voix qui n'en finit plus de les harceler dans le ciel. Oui, oublier ? Et besoin aussi, irrésistible soudain, de se laisser tomber sur cette couche d'herbes dont la vague phosphorescence, toute en molles ondulations, se fait depuis quelques secondes presque accueillante, quelle surprise, entre les troncs qui s'écartent.

Ils choient, le genou d'abord, le plat de la main, vite tout le corps, à même l'herbe trempée de pluie, mais cette pluie est tiède, c'est

ANOTHER VARIANT

They fled: the sheet of malediction plastered their bodies with its lightning and rain. Under their naked feet, the earth turned to jagged stones, slippery mud, treacherous roots. Their legs kept sliding into sinkholes, and they had to wrench them out. The boy gripped the girl's hand in his: and already, through both of them, that touch sent something more than astonishment and fear. Then she let out a scream, and toppled to the ground: and already, blood runs down her left leg, a redness new to the world. He helps her up, but her ankle won't bear any weight. Leaning on his arm, Eve can only limp through the unknown before them, the unknown around them—under this black sky of the unknown. Because it's true that night has come. How will they stagger on? Their suffering gets worse with each step; and their steps are harder and harder in this chaos, which spreads from the outside to deep inside them both. They stumble on, knowing nothing—wanting nothing but to go somewhere else, far away. Steps? More like collisions with thick limbs in the dimness, and water dumped on arms groping forward under leaves. And less a will to cross this knotted scrubland—endless, so it seems, without a rift—than to give up on the attempt: to blot out this wind, this downpour; to forget this voice in the sky, that goads them unrelentingly. Forget? Yes: but also, they can't resist a sudden urge to fling themselves on this bed of grass, whose vague phosphorescence, softly waving, has almost seemed to welcome them these last few moments, to their great surprise, between the parting trunks.

First they drop to their knees, pitching forward on their palms, and then they stretch their bodies head to toe on the rain-soaked grass; but now the rain is warm, and they receive it as a gift. They nestle

comme un don qu'on leur fait, et les voici l'un contre l'autre, très près, ce qui est le temps qui commence, avec entre eux le regard, la compassion, le désir. Lui touche du doigt cette jambe blessée, il craint d'éveiller sur ce visage si proche la grimace de la douleur, en fait il le découvre, ce visage, car l'avait-il vu, avant cet instant ? Des yeux, où l'étonnement à la fois s'accroît et se dissipe. Des lèvres. Adam et Ève se voient, se reconnaissent, se connaissent, comme on dira, c'est affaire de peu d'instants, une autre hâte, tout de même aussi un partage qui les noue l'un à l'autre vers ils ne savent où, dans une autre sorte de nuit.

Et à nouveau, bien que plus au loin, semble-t-il, ces bruits du ciel d'avant, avec des éclairs encore, un peu moins serrés, c'est possible, et dans les buissons autour de l'homme et de la femme aux aguets encore des bruits, cette fois légers, d'ailes qui s'ébrouent, de minimes vies invisibles, mais qui ne les inquiètent pas, qui les enveloppent plutôt, autre drap, car cela devient du sommeil, ce qui aussi est nouveau sur terre. Porosité de la perception, plus rien d'immobile entre dedans et dehors, des formes qui se défont, d'autres qui naissent en elles, qu'est-ce qui est, qu'est-ce qui n'est pas ?

Et de l'agitation dans ces premiers rêves mais aussi des lueurs, aux mains qui se touchent parfois, et à l'éveil c'est tout autre chose que le ciel mouvementé d'hier, ici ou là des lumières percent au travers de nuées encore grises ou noires. Ève a moins mal, c'est encourageant, elle peut se mettre debout, aller bravement de l'avant, sous cette voûte incertaine, — oui, mais d'abord ne faut-il pas réfléchir un peu à cette vie qui a commencé dans l'intimité de la nuit, cette vie autre, la vie des mots, celle des paroles, alors chuchotées et comme fiévreuses.

Et c'est Ève qui parle la première, dans un élan où je crois déceler un peu de crainte, pourquoi ?

beside each other, very close; and this is where time begins: in the look that passes between them—the compassion, the desire. He fingers her wounded leg, afraid he'll cause a wince on this face so near his own. But this face, had he ever really seen it, or does he discover it only now? Eyes, where amazement swells and fades, both at once. Lips. Adam and Eve recognize each other through that gaze; they learn how to know each other, you might say; and in a flash, a different urgency sweeps over them—a sharing, after all, that binds them to each other: toward a place they can't foretell, in another kind of night.

And once again—but farther off, it seems—they hear those rumbles from the sky; with lightning, as before, though possibly at longer intervals. The man and woman keep their ears pricked; but this time, the noises they hear in the bushes around them are faint: the whirring of wings, the scrabble of tiny, invisible lives. But these sounds don't disturb them, they envelop them: a sheet again, because it folds them into sleep, another novelty on earth. Perception seeping through the crumbled wall between the inner and the outer . . . shapes that fall apart as they give birth to other shapes . . . what is, and what is not?

There's restlessness in these first dreams, but glimmers, too; and their hands brush against each other now and then. When they wake, the stormy sky of yesterday has changed: gleams pierce the clouds here and there, though they're still gray or black. Eve has recovered, and takes heart; beneath this fitful vault, she can rise to her feet, and boldly forge ahead. But before, shouldn't they reflect a bit about this life they began in the intimate night: this other life, the life of words, whispered then as in a fever?

And it's Eve who takes the lead, with a breathlessness in which I sense a certain fear: why is that?

« Écoute, dit-elle, à voix basse, penchée sur ce visage que colorent quelques rayons, tombés du prisme des grands nuages. Écoute, hier, tu n'as pas donné tous les noms ».

Et lui : « C'est vrai. J'avais donné un nom au ruisseau. Puis j'ai vu cet élargissement qui s'était formé là où du sable s'était mêlé à des pierres et des roseaux. L'eau y passait moins rapide. Un bizarre oiseau s'était posé dans cette eau, il se tenait tout tranquille, puis il s'ébroua, s'envola, revint, pourquoi, et s'envola encore, et revint encore, et j'entendais de légers bruits sur la rive, je respirais des odeurs, était-ce la sarriette, la menthe, peu importe, ensemble tout cela existait plus que ne le faisaient chacun pour soi le sable, l'oiseau, le bruit qui bougeait sous les feuilles. Et j'ai voulu donner un nom, un seul grand nom simple, à ce moment, non, ce n'était pas un moment, à ce tout, comment dire, à cette paix. Donner un nom aussi bien à cet espace que je voyais se déformer lentement, du bleu, non, pas tout à fait du bleu, du rose tout autant, un rose d'or, entre, là-bas, deux nuages. Ou encore à ces traces pour rien que l'on voit se dessiner sur le sable, quand l'eau reflue.

Et puis il y a eu ce coup de feu, venu je ne sais d'où, et j'ai vu l'oiseau chanceler, se traîner sur le sable, et il agitait ses ailes, et le sable se soulevait, retombait sur lui, le couvrait, il eut des soubresauts, il ne bougea plus. J'ai cessé de vouloir donner des noms ».

Ève regarde ses doigts, elle joue à les écarter et les réunir. « Moi, dit-elle, je voudrais donner un nom à tout simplement cela, le noir, le noir dans les yeux, le noir quand il n'y a rien d'autre que lui, quand il n'y plus rien d'autre ».

Ils se sont mis debout. Le sang a séché le long de la jambe d'Ève tachée de boue. À doigts précautionneux elle fait tomber cette terre

"Listen," she murmurs, leaning over him. Colors stripe his face, cast by the prism of towering clouds. "Listen: yesterday, you didn't give all the names."

"True," he admits. "I'd given a name to the stream. And then I saw a place where it widened, where sand had mixed with stones and reeds, and the water flowed more sluggishly. A strange bird had alighted in that pool, and he stood perfectly still. Then he flapped his wings and flew away—but soon came back, who knows why. He flew away again, came back again, and as he did I heard low rustlings on the bank, smelled scents that seemed like savory or mint; and together, all of it existed more than anything on its own—the sand, or the bird, or the ripple of sound beneath the leaves. And I wanted to give a name, one great, simple name to this moment—not a moment, what would you call it?—a name to this whole, to this peace. And give a name to that space as well, where I saw something blue slowly shift . . . not blue, not entirely . . . pink as much as blue, a golden pink . . . over there, between two clouds. Or give a name to those aimless marks we notice on the sand, as soon as the water ebbs.

"Then gunshot rang out from who knows where, and I saw the bird totter. He dragged himself through the sand, beating his wings. The sand sprayed up and fell back, till it covered him; a few more shudders, and he lay still. I stopped wanting to give names."

Eve studies her fingers; she plays at fanning them open and shut. "As for me," she says, "I'd like to give a name to just that: the blackness. The blackness in the eyes. Black when that's all there is; when there's nothing left but black."

They stood up. On Eve's mud-smeared leg, the blood has dried; gingerly, she scrapes away that brownish dirt. Far off, the thunder still

brune. Au loin le tonnerre gronde toujours, rien de vraiment noir, des remous de couleur comme il y en aura chez des peintres. Et ce sont des averses, par grands à-coups, puis le ciel revient sur ce dont il faudra bien que les mots fassent une sorte de terre.

rumbles: no black there, really, just the swirling tones painters will use one day. Huge bursts of rain tumble down; and then the sky returns, on what words must somehow make into an earth.

FROM RATURER OUTRE

CROSSING OUT AND IN

UNE PHOTOGRAPHIE

Quelle misère, cette photographie !
Une couleur grossière défigure
Cette bouche, ces yeux. Moquer la vie
Par la couleur, c'était alors l'usage.

Mais j'ai connu celui dont on a pris
Dans ces rets le visage. Je crois le voir
Descendre dans la barque. Avec déjà
L'obole dans sa main, comme quand on meurt.

Qu'un vent se lève dans l'image, que sa pluie
La détrempe, l'efface ! Que se découvrent
Sous la couleur les marches ruisselantes !

Qui fut-il ? Qu'aura-t-il espéré ? Je n'entends
Que son pas qui se risque dans la nuit,
Gauchement, vers en bas, sans main qui aide.

A PHOTOGRAPH

This photograph is truly pathetic:
Coarse colors disfigure the mouth,
The eyes. Mocking life with color—
Back then it was par for the course.

But I knew the man whose face was caught
In this net. I seem to see him going down
Into the boat. Already with the coin
In his hand, just as when someone dies.

I want a wind to rise in this image, a rain
That will soak it, wash it away—so the steps
Beneath those colors will glisten and shine out.

Who was he? What were his hopes? All I hear
Is his footfall in the night. Awkward, he risks
His way down, and without a helping hand.

ENCORE UNE PHOTOGRAPHIE

Qui est-il, qui s'étonne, qui se demande
S'il doit se reconnaître dans cette image ?
C'est l'été, vraisemblablement, et un jardin
Où cinq ou six personnes sont réunies.

Et c'était quand, et où, et après quoi ?
Ces gens, qui furent-ils, les uns pour les autres ?
Même, s'en souciaient-ils ? Indifférents
Comme déjà leur mort leur demandait d'être.

Toutefois celui-ci, qui regarde cet autre,
Intimidé pourtant ! Étrange fleur
Que ce débris d'une photographie !

L'être pousse au hasard des rues. Une herbe pauvre
À lutter entre les façades et le trottoir.
Et ces quelques passants, déjà des ombres.

ANOTHER PHOTOGRAPH

Who is he? Astonished, he wonders:
Can that really be me in this snapshot?
Probably it's summer, in some garden
Where five or six people have gathered.

When was it, and where, and after what?
These people, who were they for each other?
Or did they even care? They seem indifferent,
Just as their death already asked them to be.

All the same, one of them darts another
An intimidated look. This photo is just
A scrap, though it's as odd as a flower.

In the streets, being grows haphazardly. A feeble
Grass, wedged between the sidewalks and facades.
And these passers-by: already no more than shades.

UN SOUVENIR

Il semblait très âgé, presque un enfant,
Il allait lentement, la main crispée
Sur un lambeau d'étoffe trempée de boue.
Ses yeux fermés, pourtant. Ah, n'est-ce pas

Que croire se souvenir est le pire leurre,
La main qui prend la nôtre pour nous perdre ?
Il me parut pourtant qu'il souriait
Lorsque bientôt l'enveloppa la nuit.

Il me parut ? Non, certes, je me trompe,
Le souvenir est une voix brisée,
On l'entend mal, même si on se penche.

Et pourtant on écoute, et si longtemps
Que parfois la vie passe. Et que la mort
Déjà dit non à toute métaphore.

A MEMORY

He looked very old, almost like a child.
He walked by slowly, his hand balled
Around a mud-soaked scrap of cloth.
And even so, his eyes were closed:

Could thinking that we remember be
The worst of lures, the hand that takes ours
To lead us astray? And yet it seemed to me
He smiled, when he vanished into the night.

Seemed to me? But no, I must be wrong.
Memory is a broken voice: we hardly
Hear it, no matter how close we lean.

Though still we listen—so long, sometimes,
That life passes us by. And already,
Death says no to all our metaphors.

LE NOM PERDU

I

Un vieil homme, à même le sol
Devant l'hôtel, à deux pas de la plage.
Il dit qu'il va mourir,
On se penche sur lui, il se détourne.

Il dit encore
Qu'il voudrait que tout vaque à son ordinaire,
Autour de lui, dans ce lieu de hasard,
Que les gens entrent et sortent,

Que les servantes chantent en dressant les tables,
Qu'elles rient avec les clients.
Et pourtant, à l'adolescent qui s'agenouille :

« Ah, prends ce livre, dit-il,
Un nom est là.
Dis-moi ce nom que je cherche. »

II

Ce livre,
Des pages déchirées qu'il tient serrées.
Deux ombres sous des vitres tachées de boue.
Peut-être est-ce le reste d'un annuaire.

THE LOST NAME

I

An old man sprawls on the ground
In front of the hotel, a stone's throw
From the beach. He says he's going to die.
People bend over him, but he turns away.

He wants them to attend to their own affairs—
As usual, he adds.
Around him, in this accidental place,
They should come and go.

The waitresses should sing while they set the tables;
They should keep on joking with the customers.
But to a young man who kneels down,

He insists: "Take this book;
A name is there.
Tell me the name I'm looking for."

II

This book:
He clutches a bunch of tattered pages. Two shadows
Under window-panes, all smudged with mud.
The remnant of a phone-book, maybe, long outdated.

Il desserre ses doigts. Des feuilles tombent.
« Rassemble-les, implore-t-il, le nom est là,
Hélas, parmi tous ces autres. » Il dit encore,
Oui, qu'il est là, qu'il l'a su.

Dans d'autres mondes
Des vagues drossent le ciel contre la terre.
Deux enfants s'éloignent sans fin sur une plage.

Il a fermé ses yeux, il tend
Ce qui lui reste du livre. « Dis-moi, dit-il,
Le nom qui consume le livre. »

III

Un nom ?
Quelque chose de rond et de lumineux,
Immobile
Comme celui de la servante de Proust.

Ah, oui ! À bout portant faire feu !
Le blesser à l'épaule, lui qui se dresse !
Qu'il tressaille, retombe
Apaisé dans la vie qui sera sans fin !

Je vois ces deux
Qui se parlent. L'un aide l'autre
À se mettre debout. Puis ils s'éloignent.

He loosens his fist; some sheets fall out.
"Pick them up," he implores. "The name is there,
There among the others." He goes on sadly
That it's there, that he knew it once.

Waves, in other worlds,
Drive the sky against the earth. On a beach, endlessly,
Two children walk away.

He's closed his eyes; now he holds up
What's left of the book. "Tell me," he says,
"The name that devours the book."

III

A name?
Something luminous and round,
Motionless
Like hers, the servant of Proust.

Yes, go ahead: fire point-blank! When he tries
To stand up, shoot him in the shoulder!
Make him wince; make him fall down
Into life without end, at peace!

I watch the two of them speaking.
One helps the other to his feet,
And then they walk away.

Le fils soutient le père, ils disparaissent
Au bout du quai, près du tas de charbon.
Leur départ, c'est étrange comme la nuit.

The father leans on his son; they vanish
At the end of the station, beside a pile of coal.
Their departure is as strange as the night.

LE PIANISTE

I

Ce clavier, il y revenait chaque matin,
C'était ainsi depuis qu'il avait cru
Entendre un son qui eût changé la vie,
Il écoutait, martelant le néant.

Et ainsi allait-il un sol détrempé.
La musique, plus rien qu'une lueur
À l'horizon d'un ciel qui restait sombre,
Il croyait que l'éclair s'y amassait.

Il vieillit. Et l'orage l'enferma
Dans sa maison aux vitres embrasées.
Ses mains sur le clavier égarèrent son rêve.

Est-il mort ? Qu'il se lève, dans le noir,
Et entrouvre sa porte, et sorte. Ne sachant
Si c'est le jour qui point ou la nuit qui tombe.

II

Une main qui se risque, désirante,
Dans les remous d'une eau soit claire soit sombre,
Son image se brise, on pourrait croire
Qu'elle n'a plus la force de retenir.

THE PIANIST

I

Every morning he came back to this
Keyboard, ever since he thought he'd heard
A sound that might have changed life itself.
He listened, hammering at nothingness.

And so he walked on sodden ground.
Music: just a gleam on the horizon
Where lightning seemed to loom,
Though the sky was always overcast.

He grew old. Inside his house, behind
Its glowing panes, the storm shut him in.
His hands lost his dream along the keys.

Is he dead? He should rise in the dark,
Open the door and go out. Not knowing
If this is day that breaks, or night that falls.

II

A hand that runs the risk of desire
In eddies of water, clear or dark:
Its shattered image makes you think
The hand must have lost its grip.

Et cette autre, dans un miroir ? Elle s'approche
De la tienne, qui vient à elle, leurs doigts se touchent
Presque, mais dans le rien de cet écart
S'ouvre l'abîme entre être et apparence.

Ces doigts, au moins, qui émeuvent des cordes.
Une autre main va-t-elle, du fond des sons,
Monter les prendre dans les siens, pour les guider ?

Mais vers quoi ? Je ne sais si c'est amour
Ou mirage, et rien que du rêve, les paroles
Qui n'ont qu'eau ou miroir, ou son, pour tenter d'être.

And this hand in the mirror? It reaches out
To yours, and yours to it: the fingers almost
Touch. But the abyss, between what is and
Only seems, now yawns in that tiniest of gaps.

What of these fingers, then, that move the strings?
Will other fingers meet them, rising from the well
Of sounds? Will they be guided by another hand?

But toward what? I cannot tell if this is love or
Just a mirage—no more than a dream: these words
That try to exist through water, mirror, or sound.

FROM L'HEURE PRÉSENTE

THE PRESENT HOUR

VOIX ENTENDUE PRÈS D'UN TEMPLE

Ils vont, dans cette campagne. Une campagne ? Non, pas vraiment. Des cailloux, des buissons épineux, une herbe dure entre de grandes plaques de pierre grise, c'est la garrigue, il n'y a jamais eu ici de cultures. Et personne non plus, à errer sur cette terre déserte.

Si déserte qu'ils sont tentés de penser qu'ils ne savent pas d'où ils viennent.

Et les voici devant quelques murs ruinés, sans doute les restes d'une bergerie. Et, c'est irrésistible, ils en franchissent la porte, étroite, envahie par les branches d'un figuier. Attends, dit-il. À deux mains, il soulève les plus basses de ces grosses branches noueuses, et son amie se penche, elle passe. Ils sont dans une salle. Le plafond est encore en place, le sol encore couvert de dalles. Les murs …

Mais ce sont des figures ! s'écrie-t-elle. En effet, sur une paroi, non, sur deux, sur trois, des hommes et des femmes, grandeur nature, debout dans le crépi qui s'écaille. Oh, effacés ! Oh, de bien peu de couleur, désormais ! À peine si du rose et du bleu sont visibles dans les effritements du vieux plâtre. Quant aux visages ! Combien y en avait-il ? Un seul peut-être. Un qui s'est élevé, au-dessus de ces corps qui semblent nus, comme une montgolfière à l'horizon d'un soir d'été, et bientôt on ne la sait plus. Sommes-nous bien sûrs de ce que nous voyons ? dit-il, ou dit-elle. Non, se disent-ils. Mais ils sont maintenant dans une autre salle. Et là un socle, avec rien dessus sauf une inscription, presque effacée.

Crois-tu que nous pourrions déchiffrer ces signes, si nous cherchions ? demande la jeune femme, agenouillée, presque nue, tout contre la pierre, sur le gravier presque rouge où il y a des brindilles. Et

VOICE HEARD NEAR A TEMPLE

They're walking in the countryside. Countryside? Not really. Rocks, thorny bushes; bristly grass, between big slabs of gray stone. This is scrubland. There were never any cultures here; and no one wanders, either, in this empty wilderness.

It's so deserted, they're tempted to believe they don't know where they came from.

And here they are before some ruined walls—the remains of a sheepfold, no doubt. It's irresistible: they have to go through the narrow door, overgrown with a fig-tree's branches. Wait, he says. With both hands, he raises the lowest of those thick, knotty branches. His friend bends down; she squeezes through. They're in a large room. The ceiling is still in place, the floor still paved with flagstones. The walls . . .

Wait, those are figures! she exclaims. It's true: on one wall—on two, on three—men and women stand erect, life-size in the flaking roughcast. They're quite faded, with very little color left; some pink and blue are barely visible in the crumbling, antique plaster. As to the faces, how many were there? Only one, perhaps. A face that has risen, above these bodies that seem nude: and like a hot-air balloon, on the horizon of a summer eve, soon it's lost from view. Are we sure about what we're seeing? he says, or she says. No, they tell each other. But now they're in another room, and here they find a pedestal. It bears nothing but an inscription, almost worn away.

Do you think we could make out these marks, if we tried? the young woman asks. Almost naked, she kneels on the reddish gravel, sprinkled with twigs, and leans against the stone. She points to a

montrant du doigt à son ami un certain groupe de lettres, six ou sept, un peu en retrait des autres. Non, je ne crois pas, répond-il. Ce ne sont pas des mots que nous ayons sus, dans nos vies. Il se penche, pourtant. Même, il s'agenouille, à son tour, il tend sa main, lui aussi … Non, n'essayons pas de comprendre. Et d'ailleurs c'est si sombre, ici. Nous sommes dans un temple, dit-elle. Nous sommes dans les ruines d'un temple.

Ils s'attardent. Ils vont d'une salle à une autre car il y en a de nombreuses. Ils vont comme ils l'auraient fait dans leurs vies. Avec maintenant du sable sous leurs pieds, dont ils aiment la chaleur. Et soudain … Ah, qu'est-ce que c'est ? s'effraie-t-elle. Il répond : Quelqu'un a crié.

— Non, pas crié, appelé.

— Appelé, non, c'était trop …

Il hésite, il ajoute : c'était trop … seul.

Et qu'il est épais, maintenant, ce silence qui entoure le temple, qui règne aussi dans ces salles, ce silence de grand été avec rien que quelques cigales et ce peu de vent qui remue des tuiles sur ce qui reste du toit !

— J'ai peur, dit-elle.

— Non, dit-il. Nous n'avons peut-être rien entendu.

Mais alors, et comme en réponse, le second de ces cris, ou de ces appels, et c'est bien plus long cette fois, une sorte de hululement où il y a de la plainte, mais aussi du très lointain, du sauvage, du triste. Quelques secondes de cette modulation, puis tout de même elle cesse. Et à nouveau si grand le silence. Si, comment dire, indéchiré. Si impénétré.

cluster of letters, six or seven, a little apart from the others. No, I don't think so, he replies. Those aren't words we've ever known—in our lives. All the same, he leans down. He even kneels in turn, and holds out his hand . . . No, let's not try to understand. Besides, it's so dark in here. We're in a temple, she says. We're in the ruins of a temple.

They linger. They go from room to room: there are a lot of them. They walk about as if they might have done this in their lives. With sand underfoot, at present; they enjoy feeling its heat. But all of a sudden . . . What's that? she starts in fear. He answers: Somebody shouted.

Not shouted, called out.

Called out—no, it was too . . .

He hesitates. He adds: It was too . . . lonely.

How dense the silence is now, this silence that surrounds the temple and reigns in the rooms as well—this silence of deep summer, with nothing but the cicadas, and puffs of wind wobbling some tiles on what's left of the roof.

I'm afraid, she says.

No, he says. Maybe we didn't hear anything.

But then, as though in response, comes the second of these cries, or these calls. And this time it's much longer—a kind of wail, like a lament; but also with a note of something far-off, something wild and sad. Even so, after a few seconds, the wail comes to an end. Again the heavy silence—how to say?—so unshattered. So unpierced.

— C'était là.

— Oui, tout près.

Ils savent que c'est dehors mais tout près. À deux pas dehors, à gauche de cette autre porte qui ouvre devant eux sur l'herbe très haute dans la lumière, une herbe désordonnée, cachant presque l'horizon des montagnes bleues. Une herbe avec des fleurs jaunes.

It was there.

Yes, very close.

They know it's outside, but very near. Just a couple of steps away, left of this other door that opens before them onto the grass, so tall in the light—rumpled grass, almost hiding the blue mountains, the horizon. Grass with yellow flowers.

BÊTE EFFRAYÉE

Ils l'ont heurtée dans ces buissons qu'ils écartaient pour se faire voie. À hauteur de leurs yeux dans les branches où elle avait grimpé, maintenant enchevêtrée dedans, prise au piège. Ils la voient, elle les regarde. Son regard est un cœur battant, une pensée.

Et voici que tu la prends dans tes mains, la retires de ce feuillage, elle ne se débat pas, dirais-tu même que tout son corps se détend ? Comme si elle se savait déjà morte, avec l'ultime recours, sous le ciel clair, c'est l'après-midi encore, d'essayer de feindre de l'être.

Morte, pour être abandonnée sur ces pierres qui n'ont pas de cesse sous leurs sandales, et là-bas, dans cette garrigue, c'est déjà un peu de la nuit.

Touche ce pelage, c'est doux. Mais attention à ces griffes !

Le pelage est le marron sombre d'une châtaigne tombée, il a même cette étroite zone de blanc qu'offrent, par en dessous, les châtaignes. Mais c'est aussi la couleur que prend maintenant le flanc de cette colline que jusqu'à présent nous suivions. Bien finies les étincellances qui bougeaient dans ses ajoncs, il y a un instant encore. Monte la terre brune sous le vert sombre et le peu de jaune et de rouge.

Et regarde ces yeux !

Les yeux sont l'énigme du monde. Car est-ce un regard, ce que tu vois dans cette vie que tu tiens dans tes mains, en commençant à te demander ce que tu vas faire d'elle, oui, lui rendre sa liberté, mais quoi d'autre, d'abord ? D'autant que ni toi ni moi ne savons lui donner de nom.

Une belette, une baleine, disait Hamlet. Ou rien que la dérive des nuages dans le ciel de la nuit maintenant tombée. Le flageolet a des

SCARED ANIMAL

They had bumped into it in the bushes they'd pushed aside to make their way. It had clambered into the branches; at eye-level now, it was entangled in them, trapped. They see it; it looks at them. Its gaze is a beating heart, a thought.

And here you take it in your hands, you pull it out of the foliage. It doesn't struggle: could you even say its whole body goes slack? As though it knew it was already dead; and as a last resort, under the limpid sky of late afternoon, it must try to play dead.

Dead, so they'll leave it behind on these stones, stretching off endlessly under their sandals. And over there, in that scrubland, there's already a hint of night.

Touch this fur, it's soft. But watch out for those claws!

The fur is deep brown, like a fallen chestnut; it even has the narrow white mark shown by chestnuts underneath. But it's also the color that tinges this hillside now, the one we've been following all along. Gone are the sparkles that skittered through the gorse, till just a moment ago. The umber earth swells under the dark green, with smidgeons of yellow and red.

And look at those eyes!

Eyes are the enigma of the world. Is this really a gaze you see, in the life you hold in your hands? You start to wonder what you're going to do with it. Let it loose again, no doubt; but before that, what else? Since neither you nor I know how to give it a name.

A weasel, a whale, Hamlet said. Or nothing but the clouds adrift in the sky, now that night has fallen. The recorder has stops our fingers

trous sur lesquels nos doigts ne savent pas se poser ! Une belette, dis-tu, un furet ? Qu'est-ce qu'un furet, qu'est-ce qu'un blaireau ? Je voudrais connaître les noms, dis-tu. Moi je voudrais en imaginer, mais le langage est aussi fermé sur ses ajoncs et ses pierres que le sol de cette colline, tout près de nous, même sous nos pieds. Et je ne vois même plus, si, tout de même un peu, ces petits yeux, ce regard.

Et brusquement la bête se débat, se libère presque. Et tu resserres tes mains, tes doigts. Elle est à nouveau tout immobile.

Va la poser sur cette pierre, là, devant nous. Cette pierre qui brille un peu, car voici que la lune s'est levée, elle a quelques lueurs pour cet affleurement du rocher, une étendue presque nue, et plate, bien qu'elle ait des bosses mais légères. On croirait la table d'un sacrifice.

Je touche le dos de la bête, ne dois-je pas lui dire adieu, avant qu'elle ne s'échappe, dans ce monde qui ne nous a pas enseigné tous les mots qu'il faudrait, tous les gestes qui délivreraient ?

Et déjà tu te penches, mais nous sursautons, l'un et l'autre, un cri a été poussé, là-bas, près de ces ruines où nous étions, tout à l'heure. Un cri, puis, nous écoutons, quel silence, et à nouveau c'est lui, et qui se prolonge, ce hululement, puis s'arrête.

C'est le même, nous disons-nous. Et de même qu'auprès du temple, nous avons peur.

Mais rien, rien d'autre, rien de plus dans le silence de là-bas et de toutes parts, ce silence qui fait corps avec ce qu'il y a de nuit tout autour de nous, et en nous. Car c'est vrai, je l'ai déjà dit, qu'il fait nuit maintenant, sauf toutefois sur cette petite étendue de pierre grise, presque brillante.

Distraitement tu as posé sur la pierre la bête qui est sans mouvement. Et d'un bond elle se déploie et déjà elle a disparu dans les broussailles sombres voisines.

aren't able to play. A weasel, you say, a ferret? What's a ferret, what's a badger? I'd like to learn the names, you say. As for me, I'd like to make them up. But language is as closed on its gorse-bushes and stones as the ground of this hill, right next to us, under our very feet. And I don't even see those small eyes anymore, that gaze—yes I do, after all, just a bit.

Suddenly the creature thrashes, almost wriggles loose. And you squeeze it tighter with your fingers, your hands. Again it goes limp.

Lay it down on that rock over there, in front of us. The rock that's gleaming a little, since the moon has risen now: the moon has a few glowing touches for this outcrop of stone. It's a surface that's almost bare—and flat, though with some gentle humps. A sacrificial table, you might think.

I stroke the creature's back. Shouldn't I say good-bye before it escapes? In this world that hasn't taught us all the words we might need—all the gestures that might deliver us.

And you're already leaning down—but both of us jump back: we've heard a cry from over there, near those ruins where we were a while ago. A cry, and then we listen. What a silence . . . Then we hear the cry again, a wail that lasts longer this time, then stops.

It's the same, we say to ourselves. And just as near the temple, we're afraid.

But nothing: nothing more in the silence over there and everywhere, this silence at one with the night all around us—and in us. As I've said, it's true that night has fallen now, except on this short expanse of gray stone, almost shimmering.

Distractedly, you've laid the inert creature on the rock. And with a bound, it vanishes into the somber underbrush nearby.

PREMIÈRE ÉBAUCHE D'UNE MISE EN SCÈNE D'*HAMLET*

Cette mise en scène n'avait eu qu'un vœu, disait-on, se conformer aux exigences du texte.

Par exemple, quand les guetteurs échangent leurs premiers mots, le metteur en scène n'a cherché qu'à faire paraître la nuit comme ces soldats l'éprouvent sur ces remparts, dans le froid. Un froid qui règne aussi dans la salle, si ce lieu de l'écoute, c'est une salle. Les spectateurs qui sont là quand j'arrive sont pelotonnés dans leurs vêtements qui les gardent parfois presque étendus sur le sol, et c'est avec prudence que je dois mettre le pied dans d'étroits espaces entre les corps dont je vois beaucoup la laine des manteaux, sur le sable clair, bien plus rarement la soie des robes. En vérité, c'est comme si ces hommes, ces femmes — fort peu d'enfants —, sont arrivés il y a déjà nombre de jours, ou plutôt de nuits. Car ils ont allumé des feux qui de loin en loin percent de leurs fumées rouges l'obscurité qui est sans limites. Et certains dorment, j'entends des souffles réguliers, paisibles, mais je croise aussi des regards qui sont, eux, aux aguets, perçants, ils me font peur, je me hâte. Au loin, à des moments, de ces cris que l'on ne pousse qu'en rêve. Je vais, hésitant, revenant sur mes pas, gardant toutefois mes yeux fixés sur la scène.

La scène ? Elle est vaguement éclairée, j'y distingue pourtant de très hauts rochers, de la pluie, et quatre ou cinq hommes ou femmes qui s'affairent autour d'une table sur laquelle est posé un livre. L'un prend le livre, regarde la page où il est ouvert. « Je lis, dit-il, Who's there ? » Exclamations confuses, autour de lui. L'autre grand vœu du metteur en scène, en effet, c'est de comprendre le texte. Oui, d'abord, d'en prendre chacun des mots à la lettre, mais aussi de découvrir tout

FIRST SKETCH FOR A STAGING OF *HAMLET*

This staging, they said, had only one aim: to stick to the requirements of the text.

For example, when the watchmen exchange their opening words, the director simply tried to make the night like what the soldiers feel on those ramparts, out in the cold. A cold that pervades the theater as well—if this place where we're listening is a theater. The spectators who're already here when I arrive are huddled in heavy clothes: sometimes they're almost spread out on the ground, so I have to step with care in the crannies between their bodies. On the light-colored sand, I mostly see the wool of overcoats; and much less often, the silk of dresses. Actually, I'd say these men and women, along with a handful of children, must have gotten here a number of days ago—or rather nights ago. They've lit fires here and there: their ruddy smoke pierces the boundless dark. Some of these people are asleep; I hear their regular, peaceful breathing. But I come across others who're on the lookout, and whose penetrating stares frighten me so much I hurry on. Far off, from time to time, I hear the kind of shouts we only let out in dreams. I walk gingerly, backtracking as I go, though always keeping my eyes trained on the stage.

The stage? It's dimly lit, but I can still make out the towering rocks, the rain, and four or five men or women, milling around a table with a book on top. One of them picks it up and looks at the page it's opened to. "I read," he says: "Who's there?" Around him, muddled cries. As it happens, the director's other main goal is to grasp the text: in the first place, to follow each word literally, but also to unearth what each word means. How should he go about it, in the thick of this night? It seems

le sens de ce qu'ils disent. Et comment le faire, dans cette nuit ? Les assistants du metteur en scène, ces êtres vagues qui se serrent autour de lui, ne sont d'accord ni avec lui ni entre eux, me semble-t-il. « Qui vient-là ? » Certes, comment savoir qui vient là ?

« Et qu'est-il dit ensuite ? », s'écrie quelqu'un. « Friends to this ground », répond quelqu'un d'autre. Sur quoi un troisième se penche, ramasse sur le sol une grosse pierre, la soulève à grand peine, écarte ses amis, tente de la jeter, loin. Si l'acteur jetait cette pierre, demande-t-il, est-ce que cela aurait quelque sens ? Attention, lui répond une jeune femme. Tu es un des acteurs, n'oublie pas, et le spectacle est commencé, déjà. Il l'est depuis des heures, des jours.

Mais soudain beaucoup d'agitation dans la salle, on se lève de toutes parts, on s'étire, on s'exclame, on se met en mouvement parce que l'on vient de comprendre qu'en fait la représentation a lieu ailleurs aussi, ailleurs autant qu'ici, et par exemple, en ce moment même, dans un chalet d'altitude qu'il faut rejoindre par un étroit sentier où à des endroits il a neigé et restent des flaques. Ce chalet, une de ces constructions de bois léger un peu coucou suisse, comme on aimait en placer au fond de la scène des grands théâtres aux siècles de bel canto. Il faudra en pousser la porte, aventurer son regard dans cette chambre éclairée — une lampe sur une table —, voir là Hamlet insultant sa mère. Gertrude ? Oui, écroulée sur un lit, ses épaules nues, tous ses cheveux en désordre. Elle cache sa tête dans sa main. « Ne m'accable pas », gémit-elle. Hélas, qui va s'intéresser à son sort ? Le bruit court maintenant qu'un peu plus haut sur ce même chemin le metteur en scène a pris *Hamlet* par un autre bout. Belle et noble façade cette fois, tout en pierre, et des colonnes en haut des marches avec sur la dernière de celle-ci deux êtres indéchiffrables que je vois —

to me that his assistants, vague beings who cluster around him, don't agree with him or with each other. "Who's there?" Admittedly, how can you know who's there?

"And what comes after that?" somebody exclaims. "Friends to this ground," somebody else replies. At that, a third bends over and raises a big stone from the ground. He has a hard time lifting it; he elbows his friends aside and tries to toss it fairly far off. "If the actor threw this rock," he asks, "would that have any meaning?" "Hold on," a young woman answers him. "You are one of the actors, don't forget, and the show has already started. It's been going on for hours, for days."

But all of a sudden, there's a great hubbub in the theater. All over the place, people are standing up, stretching their limbs, and talking out loud. They're on the move, since they've just realized the performance is going on elsewhere as well, elsewhere as much as here: for example, at this very moment, in a mountain chalet that can only be reached by climbing a narrow path, where snowfalls have left some puddles along the way. The chalet is one of those light wooden constructions, a bit like a Swiss cuckoo-clock—the kind big theaters liked to place upstage in the bel canto era. You'll have to open the door and venture to look into this room, illumined by a table lamp; inside, you'll see Hamlet insulting his mother. Gertrude? Yes, collapsed on a bed, her shoulders bared, her hair disheveled. She's hiding her head with one of her hands. "O, speak to me no more," she groans. What a shame—but who's interested in her fate? News spreads that somewhat farther up on this same path, the director has taken another tack with *Hamlet.* This time there's a noble, handsome facade made from stone, with columns at the top of the stairs. On the highest step, I—at any rate—see two unreadable beings; they struggle silently, bare palms

moi, en tout cas — lutter silencieusement, mains nues de l'un appliquées à plat contre les mains nues de l'autre. Depuis quand cet affrontement, et pendant combien d'heures, combien de nuits, va-t-il continuer ? Est-ce cela, « readiness », cela, le triste vœu qui tourbillonne et se creuse dans le gouffre de la parole ? Au-dessus de ce vain combat la paroi rocheuse, le vent froid.

Et il y a tant d'autres scènes ! Et les spectateurs savent si bien qu'il faut partir à leur découverte, même loin dans ces sortes de moraines, sous ces sapins enneigés, poussant, bravement, des portes derrière lesquelles, parfois, ce sont des cris, déchirants. Le théâtre est grand comme la montagne. Le théâtre est la montagne. Ophélie y erre, pieds nus. On la regarde passer, on s'écarte, elle est seule, elle chantonne à des moments, sa solitude est si grande !

Quel travail, cette mise en scène d'*Hamlet* ! Que de tentations, pour le maître d'œuvre, que de désirs à repousser mais à comprendre, d'abord, comprendre ! Par exemple : qu'est-ce que cet enfant qui pleure au bord de la route ? Un vieux sage en robe de voyageur, c'est Bashô, le bienveillant, s'arrête auprès de lui, pose sa main sur son épaule, le questionne, l'écoute, hoche la tête, s'éloigne. Et qu'est-ce que cette deuxième jeune fille, peu vêtue, qui nourrit de grands oiseaux noirs dans une sorte d'étable, où on entend des chevaux piétiner dans l'ombre, parfois hennir ? On dit que dans la mise en scène d'*Hamlet* c'est l'auteur lui-même, redevenu l'acteur qu'il avait été, qui est requis de venir vers elle, par un long chemin à travers les pierres du temps, les voix de l'espace. Il approche, on ne sait pas où il est au juste, peut-être va-t-il paraître en quelque point de la vaste scène, en mains une lampe-tempête, sur son visage le masque que sont les mots de la poésie.

against bare palms. When did this face-off begin, and how many hours, how many nights, will it persist? Is this "readiness"? Is this the sad vow that whirls and burrows down, deep in the abyss of words? And above this vain combat: the wall of rock, the frigid wind.

There are so many other scenes! The spectators know very well they must set out to find them, even far away in what seem like moraines. Beneath snow-covered firs, they must boldly open doors—though behind them, heart-rending cries can sometimes be heard. The theater is as huge as the mountain. The theater is the mountain. Ophelia wanders around it barefoot. We watch her go by; we stand back. She's all alone, humming to herself: her solitude is so immense . . .

What a lot of work, this staging of *Hamlet!* The set builder faces untold temptations, endless desires he must discard; but first he must understand them. For example: what should we make of this child who's weeping at the edge of the road? An old sage in traveling dress—it's Basho, always benevolent—stops beside the boy and lays his hand on his shoulder; he questions him, listens, nods his head, and walks on. And who's this second young woman? Scantily clad, she feeds some large black birds in a kind of stable; in the shadows, we hear horses stamp, neighing now and then. We're told that in this staging of *Hamlet*, the author himself has become an actor again, the actor he once was. He's required to come toward her on a lengthy path, across the stones of time, the voices of space. He keeps moving closer, though we don't know exactly where he is. Maybe he'll appear at some point on the enormous stage, a hurricane lamp in his hands: and the mask on his face will be the words of poetry.

HAMLET EN MONTAGNE

On avait annoncé une représentation d'*Hamlet* en montagne.

C'était dire que l'on ressentait fortement, là-haut, qu'il faut qu'on sache que d'énormes masses de pierre environnent de toujours dans la pensée de Shakespeare le prince de Danemark. Roches qui le surplombent ou se pressent autour de lui, failles qui s'ouvrent entre elles, d'où suit que sa voix ne sera jamais perçue qu'au loin, presque couverte presque toujours par le bruit de torrents dévalant des pentes sous les cris des oiseaux de ces autres mondes.

Et le public, à peine franchie la billetterie, une petite guérite à un début de sentier sous une large falaise, aura donc à se déplacer sans cesse. Pourquoi, au vrai ? Est-ce parce que les diverses scènes de la pièce ont été disséminées, sans souci de chronologie, en autant de lieux de la montagne ? Certains auraient préféré cette conception, parmi ceux qui avaient pris autrefois la responsabilité de la représentation. Il y en avait eu pour vouloir qu'Hamlet insultât sa mère dans une ferme qu'il y avait sur un des alpages. À la lueur de bougies que des domestiques auraient porté ça et là dans une des salles, mouvementant sur les murs de longues ombres portées, il l'eût traînée par les cheveux, jetée sur un lit, bientôt s'écroulant en pleurs à ses genoux qu'auraient découverts ses mains fiévreuses. Et peut-être y a-t-il, dans quelque combe à l'écart de tout, des acteurs à jouer ainsi, à vivre ainsi, à vieillir de cette façon funèbre dans l'inépuisable parole, d'autres scènes se déroulant ailleurs, s'y achevant puis recommençant. Mais non, disait d'autres, ce n'est pas ce que la montagne veut de Shakespeare.

Et de fait ! Les spectateurs passent le seuil étroit du théâtre, ils

HAMLET IN THE MOUNTAINS

They'd announced a performance of *Hamlet* in the mountains.

Up there it was strongly felt people should know what enormous masses of stone always surround the Prince of Denmark, in Shakespeare's mind. Rock walls that tower above him or huddle around him, faults that fissure between them. So his voice will never reach us except from afar, almost muffled by torrents hurtling down a precipice, while birds from those other worlds screech overhead.

As for the audience, as soon as they pass the box office—a small hut at a trail-head beneath a sweeping cliff—they'll have to move on without letup. Why is that? Because the play's various scenes have been dispersed, regardless of sequence, over an equal number of places in the mountains? Among those who once sponsored the performance, some would have preferred that approach. There had been support for having Hamlet berate his mother at a farm on the high-range meadows. Casting long shadows on the walls, servants would carry candles to and fro through one of the rooms; in their glow, he'd drag her by the hair and throw her on a bed. Soon he'd collapse in tears, his frantic hands fumbling at her knees. And maybe, in some far-flung valley, actors exist who play like that, live like that, grow old in the gloom of inexhaustible speech, with other scenes unfolding elsewhere, ending there and beginning again. Oh no, said others; that's not what the mountains want from Shakespeare.

No doubt about it: spectators keep on crossing the theater's narrow

avancent, pressés les uns contre les autres, on croirait à l'infini, tâtonnant, trébuchant, presque à en tomber, dans cette nuit noire ; et là-bas, en avant, que se passe-t-il ? « Une altercation entre deux personnes », crie un jeune homme qui, non sans créer grand désordre, accourt vers moi à contre-courant dans la foule. « Et l'une a pris l'autre au collet, elle la secoue, vocifère ». Qu'est-ce que cela signifie, je veux le savoir, je presse le pas, je fraye mon chemin entre des dos qui s'écartent de mauvais gré sous leurs parapluies, car il pleut, le froid tombe aussi du ciel. Mais c'est bien en vain que j'ai tenté cet effort. L'aval de ce flux ne s'ouvre guère, l'amont piétinant et murmurant ne cesse de m'engluer, je suis rejeté sur un chemin latéral où, c'est étonnant, il n'y a maintenant presque personne.

Quelques pas sur ce chemin de sable très clair, avec des flaques, et voici que deux hommes viennent dans ma direction, ils vont me croiser, ils se parlent. J'entends même que l'un dit à l'autre, pensivement, quand ils passent auprès de moi : « What's Hecuba to him, or he to Hecuba ? »

Et je comprends. Les scènes d'*Hamlet* ne sont pas dispersées dans la montagne, ce sont les acteurs qui l'ont été dans la foule. Et ces scènes en sont brisées, l'action s'est défaite, mais au milieu des spectateurs qui affluent toujours plus nombreux va peut-être se rassembler, prendre forme, crier son sens sans même aucun personnage du drame à proximité immédiate, la grande scène introuvable dans l'œuvre en son simple texte.

Je comprends cette pensée. Et ce désir, je l'approuve : d'autant que pour que l'action ainsi fragmentée soit au même degré de densité que ce piétinement qui n'a plus d'origine et va avancer sans fin, il a bien fallu que le metteur en scène en fait omniprésent multiplie les acteurs

threshold; they press by, closely packed, so many they seem infinite. They grope forward, stumbling, almost falling down in the blackness of this night. But there, up ahead, what's going on? "Two people are arguing," a young man exclaims, running toward me against the current—which causes mayhem in the crowd. "One of them grabbed the other by the collar; he's shaking him and shouting." I want to know what it's all about, so I wedge past backs that testily shift aside beneath umbrellas—rain is falling from the sky, and a chill as well. But I've gone to all this trouble in vain. The onward flow hardly admits any leeway, and the trudging, clamorous host overwhelms me. I'm shunted off on a side path, where I'm surprised to find almost no one now.

After a few steps along this trail of light-colored sand, with puddles here and there, I see two men coming in my direction. Our paths are about to cross, and they're talking to each other. As they walk by me, I even hear one of them say, pensively: "What's Hecuba to him, or he to Hecuba?"

Now I understand. The scenes of *Hamlet* aren't strewn over the mountains: it's the players who're scattered through the crowd. This has broken up the scenes, unraveling the action. On the other hand, among these spectators streaming by in ever-larger droves, perhaps another scene will come to a head and take shape—will cry out its meaning, even without the drama's characters nearby—the great scene that can't be found in the work's unvarnished text.

I grasp this thought, and I applaud this desire: all the more since the action, blown apart like that, demands the same kind of density as this tramping which has lost all origin, and which will never end. The director—omnipresent in fact—has been obliged to multiply the ac-

à l'instant même où il les disperse, si bien que dans le flot mouvant, turbulent, de cette multitude étonnée, il en a lancé de nombreux pour jouer Hamlet, de nombreux pour Polonius ou l'étonnante Gertrude, de nombreux tout autant pour Laërte ou pour Ophélie. D'où suit que ce ne sont pas seulement ces hommes d'ici et ces femmes, mais autant d'Hamlet, autant de Polonius, de Claudius, autant même de Rosencrantz et de Guildenstern, qui, désormais des êtres réels, plus ou moins, du fait des variations dans la figure, de beaux visages parfois, ou des gestes fous, qu'ici ou là on leur prête, erreront indéfiniment dans cette foule hagarde sur les terrasses herbeuses de leur immense Elseneur. Chacun pour suivre une idée de soi que celui qui le représente sert, habilement, mais trop souvent sans pouvoir trouver les mots pour la dire. Chacun s'étonnant d'être ce qu'il est, chacun s'effrayant de ces grandes roches qui tantôt ne permettent que le plus étroit des passages, tantôt semblent s'écarter, avec majesté, mais sur un au-delà qui a des rumeurs de gave grondant à jamais au fond d'un gouffre.

Je vais, sur un chemin de traverse, un peu au-dessus du gros de ce courant qui par mille voies cherche à traverser la montagne ; et qui, là où je suis, s'est réduit, pour l'instant, à rien que quelques personnes.

Un gros homme me dépasse, en riant.

Et voici qu'il y a devant moi, arrêtés, une dizaine d'hommes, de femmes. Ils font cercle, que regardent-ils ? Je me glisse parmi eux.

C'est Ophélie. Elle est assise sur une pierre, son parapluie auprès d'elle, la tête penchée sur une sorte de sac à mains dans lequel elle cherche, avec une visible inquiétude. Bien peu vêtue, presque nue, cette jeune fille, une pauvre robe trouée de laine noire comme prise au hasard à quelque réveil dans un trop grand rêve. Et on voit bien qu'elle a froid ; que ses mains tremblent. Va-t-elle tirer de son sac,

tors, at the very moment he's dispersed them. That's why he's sent a wave of them into the surging, turbulent swell of this bewildered horde. Many play Hamlet, many play Polonius or the amazing Gertrude, just as many play Laertes or Ophelia. It follows that a huge number of the men and women here aren't what they appear; instead, they're Hamlet, Polonius, Claudius, even Rosencrantz and Guildenstern—swarms of them. From now on, their varied features make them into real beings, more or less. With beautiful faces at times, or mad gestures here and there, they'll wander through this dazed throng indefinitely, on the grassy terraces of their immense Elsinore. All pursue certain concepts of their personae, skillfully molded by those who portray them; though often, they can't find the words to express their intent. All feel stunned by being who they are; all are frightened by these gigantic boulders, which either funnel them into cramped passages, or seem to draw apart, majestically—on a beyond that roars like a stream down below, rumbling forever in the abyss.

I file up a side path, a little higher than the multitude, which is trying to traverse this mountain by a thousand different tracks; here where I am, the crowd has dwindled now to just a few people.

Laughingly, a fat man passes me.

And there before me, a dozen men and women have come to a halt. They stand in a circle, but what are they looking at? I slip in among them.

It's Ophelia. She's sitting on a rock, her umbrella beside her. Her head is bent over a sort of handbag; she's looking for something inside it, visibly distressed. The young woman is hardly dressed, almost nude; her shabby garment of black wool is full of holes. It looks like she must've put it on at random, after waking up from too long a dream. You can tell she's cold: her hands are trembling. Is she going to pull

abîmés, flétris, le fenouil, le romarin, l'ancolie que le poète a voulu qu'elle offre au monde qui n'entend rien et ne comprend pas ? Mais non, tout brusquement elle se relève et la tête toujours penchée, le sac et le parapluie serrés maintenant contre son corps, se jette en avant, un peu titubante. Où va-t-elle ? Qu'a-t-elle dit ? Où dois-je aller, désormais ?

Heures, heures que nous passerons à monter vers cette cime qui parfois, à des détours, se laisse entrevoir, illuminée par la lune, indifférente. Des routes s'ouvrent, beaucoup d'entre nous les ont déjà prises, d'autres hésitent encore. Le vent ne cesse pas, il ne cessera pas, on le comprend bien, même la vie ne cessera pas : être ici, c'est avoir à ne pas cesser de vivre. Et voici d'ailleurs qu'un cavalier se fraye voie parmi mes proches d'en ce moment, son cheval hennit, un cheval noir, il se cabre, l'acteur, est-ce un acteur, qui le chevauche, est revêtu d'une armure, c'est certainement le vieil Hamlet, le roi mort. Mais pourquoi l'a-t-on affublé de cette écharpe vaguement rouge, par-dessus sa cotte de maille ? Le vent la soulève fort joliment, il est vrai ; autour de cette tête chenue elle a de beaux mouvements de jeune écriture. Et qu'elle est longue, cette banderole, on pourrait la croire sans fin et qu'elle se perd déjà parmi ces étoiles qu'on voit encore, Dieu sait pourquoi, bien que plus que jamais il vente et pleuve.

something withered and spoiled out of her bag—the fennel, the rosemary, the columbine? The poet had wanted her to proffer them, to a world that won't listen or understand. But wait. All of a sudden she gets up, her head still bowed, clutching the bag and umbrella to her body. She plunges ahead, tottering a bit. Where is she headed? What did she say? Where should I go from here?

We'll spend hours and hours climbing toward that summit. Sometimes, around a bend, we catch sight of it—glimmering in the moonlight, indifferent. Roads widen before us; many of us have already taken them, while others still hesitate. The wind doesn't stop, and it won't stop, we realize. Even life won't stop; being here means this: that we can't stop living. By way of proof, here's a rider making his way through the people who're beside me at the moment. His black horse whinnies and rears up. The actor in the saddle—assuming he's an actor—wears armor: he must be the older Hamlet, the dead king. But why did they deck him out in this reddish scarf, on top of his coat of mail? True, the wind sails it up very handsomely; around his hoary head, it traces lovely strokes of youthful writing. The streamer is so long you could almost believe it's endless—that it trails off into those stars we still see, God knows why, though the wind and rain lash harder than ever.

SELECT BIBLIOGRAPHY

Books by Yves Bonnefoy Translated into English

The Act and the Place of Poetry: Selected Essays. Edited and with an introduction by John T. Naughton; foreword by Joseph Frank. Chicago: University of Chicago Press, 1989.

The Beginning and the End of the Snow (*Début et fin de la neige*). Translated by John T. Naughton and Richard Stamelman. In *New and Selected Poems.*

The Curved Planks (*Les planches courbes*). Translated and with an afterword by Hoyt Rogers; foreword by Richard Howard. New York: Farrar, Straus and Giroux, 2006.

Derniers raisins de Zeuxis / The Last Grapes of Zeuxis. Translated by Richard Stamelman. Montauk: Monument Press, 1993.

Early Poems, 1947–1959. Translated by Galway Kinnell and Richard Pevear. Athens: Ohio University Press, 1991.

Encore les raisins de Zeuxis / Once More the Grapes of Zeuxis. Translated by Richard Stamelman. Montauk: Monument Press, 1990.

L'horizon / The Horizon. Translated by Michael Bishop. Halifax: Editions VVV Editions, 2003. [At Editions VVV Editions, Bishop has also published his translations of several other short works by Bonnefoy.]

In the Lure of the Threshold (*Dans le leurre du seuil*). Translated by John T. Naughton. In *Temenos* 6, 1985.

In the Shadow's Light (*Ce qui fut sans lumière*). Translated by John Naughton; with an interview with Bonnefoy. Chicago: University of Chicago Press, 1991.

In the Threshold's Lure (*Dans le leurre du seuil*). Translated by Yves Bonnefoy. Montauk: Monument Press, 2001.

The Lure of the Threshold (*Dans le leurre du seuil*). Translated by Richard Pevear. In *Poems, 1959–1975*.

The Lure and the Truth of Painting: Selected Essays on Art. Edited, with an introduction and afterword, by Richard Stamelman; preface by Yves Bonnefoy. Chicago: University of Chicago Press, 1995.

Mythologies. Edited by Yves Bonnefoy; translated under the direction of Wendy Doniger. 2 vols. Chicago: University of Chicago Press, 1991.

New and Selected Poems. Edited by John Naughton and Anthony Rudolf. Chicago: University of Chicago Press, 1995.

On the Motion and Immobility of Douve (*Du mouvement et de l'immobilité de Douve*). Translated by Galway Kinnell. Athens: Ohio University Press, 1968; repr., Northumberland: Bloodaxe Books, 1992. [Also in *Early Poems, 1947–1959*.]

The Origin of Language and Other Poems. Translated by Susanna Lang. Montauk: Monument Press, 1979.

Poems, 1959–1975. Translated by Richard Pevear. New York: Random House, 1985.

The Primacy of Gaze: Some Remarks about Raymond Masson / La primauté du regard : quelques regards sur Raymond Masson. Translated by Anthony Rudolf. Birmingham: Delos Press, 2000.

Les raisins de Zeuxis et d'autres fables / The Grapes of Zeuxis and Other Fables. Translated by Richard Stamelman. Montauk: Monument Press, 1987.

Selected Poems. Translated by Anthony Rudolf. London: Jonathan Cape/Grossman, 1969.

Shakespeare and the French Poet. Edited and with an introduction by John Naughton, with an interview with Yves Bonnefoy. Chicago: University of Chicago Press, 2004.

Things Dying, Things Newborn: Selected Poems. Translated by Anthony Rudolf. London: Menard Press, 1985.
Traité du pianiste. Translated by Anthony Rudolf. Birmingham: Delos Press, 1994.
Transmorphosis. Translated by Richard Stamelman. Montauk: Monument Press, 1997.
Words in Stone (*Pierre écrite*). Translated by Susanna Lang. Amherst: University of Massachusetts Press, 1976.
Written Stone (*Pierre écrite*). Translated by Richard Pevear. In *Poems, 1959–1975.*
Yesterday's Empty Kingdom (*Hier régnant désert*). Translated by Richard Pevear. In *Poems,* 1959–1975.
Yesterday's Wilderness Kingdom (*Hier régnant désert*). Translated by Anthony Rudolf. London: MPT Books, 2000.

Other Books by Yves Bonnefoy (with Proposed Titles in English)

Dans un débris de miroir (*In a Shard of Mirror*). Paris: Galilée, 2006.
La longue chaîne de l'ancre (*The Anchor's Long Chain*). Paris: Mercure de France, 2008.
L'arrière-pays (*The Hinterland*). Geneva: Skira, 1972.
La vie errante (*The Wandering Life*). Paris: Mercure de France, 1993.
L'heure présente (*The Present Hour*). Paris: Mercure de France, 2011.
L'improbable (*The Improbable*). Paris: Mercure de France, 1959.
Raturer outre (*Crossing Out and In*). Paris: Galilée, 2010.
Une autre époque de l'écriture (*Another Era of Writing*). Paris: Mercure de France, 1988.